# Protecting Your
# Identity

*If you want to know how . . .*

7 Ways to Build Your Pension
How To Deal with Death and Probate
How To Earn Money in Retirement
How To make Your Own Will
How To Pay Less for More
How To Save Inheritance Tax
Investing in Stocks and Shares
Seven Ways for Anyone to Boost Their Income
Spending the Kids' Inheritance
The Personal Security Handbook
Your Retirement Masterplan

**howto**books

Please send for a free copy of the latest catalogue:

How To Books
Spring Hill House, Spring Hill Road,
Begbroke, Oxford OX5 1RX, United Kingdom
Tel: (01865) 375794. Fax: (01865) 379162.
info@howtobooks.co.uk
www.howtobooks.co.uk

# Protecting Your
# Identity

## A Practical Guide to Preventing Identity Theft and its Damaging Consequences

MATTHEW RECORD

**howto**books

Published by How To Books Ltd,
Spring Hill House, Spring Hill Road,
Begbroke, Oxford OX5 1RX, United Kingdom
Tel: (01865) 375794. Fax: (01865) 379162
info@howtobooks.co.uk
www.howtobooks.co.uk

How To Books greatly reduce the carbon footprint of their books by sourcing their typesetting and printing in the UK.

British Library Cataloguing in Publication Data
A catalogue record for this book is available from the British Library

ISBN 978 1 84528 253 0

Produced for How To Books by Deer Park Productions, Tavistock
Typeset by PDQ Typesetting Ltd, Newcastle-under-Lyme
Printed and bound by Cromwell Press Ltd, Trowbridge, Wiltshire

NOTE: The material contained in this book is set out in good faith for general guidance and no liability can be accepted for loss or expense incurred as a result of relying in particular circumstances on statements made in the book. The laws and regulations are complex and liable to change, and readers should check the current position with the relevant authorities before making personal arrangements.

# Contents

# Preface

Your identity is the single most important commodity that you own and it must be protected at all times. It is used to prove who you are, where you live and what credit rating you have. This information is a necessary and fundamental part of everyday modern life, but at present it cannot be proven with a single document or a single means of identification. This is because different organisations use different documents to confirm who you are and, unfortunately, these can be easily stolen, forged or altered to create a false identity or to steal an existing one.

If you become a victim of identity theft, reclaiming your identity and restoring your financial status can be a lengthy, time-consuming and emotionally draining experience. However, with a little forethought and careful planning, a number of simple preventive steps can be taken to reduce the possibility of this happening. This book explores what identity theft is and provides practical advice about how to protect yourself from its damaging consequences.

*Matthew Record*

# (1)

# What is Identity Theft?

Identity theft is just one of many identity-related crimes but because of the media coverage it generates it is often perceived as the only identity-related crime. This book will explain the differences between the various types of identity crimes and will offer practical advice about how to protect yourself, what to do if your identity is stolen, and where to get further help.

Identity fraud is the UK's fastest growing crime. It affects individuals, government departments and private sector organisations and is estimated to currently cost the UK economy around £2 billion per annum. With just a few of your personal details, criminals can open bank accounts, buy expensive goods, claim benefits, obtain credit cards, loans and mortgages and apply for passports and driving licences – all in your name. They can also claim the identity of deceased people, including children, which can be extremely distressing to family members.

Your identity is extremely valuable and should be safe-guarded at all times, but most people are unaware of how easily it can be stolen or compromised. If you do become a victim, then reclaiming your identity and restoring your financial status can be a lengthy, time-consuming and emotionally draining experience. Fortunately, there are a number of simple preventive steps that you can take to protect it from criminals.

## TYPES OF IDENTITY CRIME

There are many ways that your identity can be stolen and there are many ways that your identity can be used. This can often lead to confusion when attempting to differentiate between the various types of identity-related crimes. To help clarify the situation, the Home Office Identity Fraud Steering Committee (IFSC) has developed a series of definitions as follows.

### Identity crime

This encompassing term is used to describe the three main types of identity related crime that are committed against private individuals. These are identity theft, creating a false identity and committing identity fraud. Criminals and fraudsters use a combination of scams and schemes to commit identity crime and these will be explored throughout this book.

### Identity theft

Identity theft occurs when criminals acquire enough of your personal details to either assume your entire identity or to create a new and fictitious identity based on your details. This information includes:

- your name
- date of birth
- current or previous address
- mother's maiden name
- National Insurance Number.

For further information, see page 12, How Your Personal Information Is Used.

## False identity theft

As the name implies, a false identity is one that has never existed before. This can be created in one of two ways: either a completely new identity can be produced from counterfeit documents or a fictitious identity can be created from genuine documents that have been altered. A false identity can be used to:

- hide from the authorities
- avoid existing legal and financial obligations
- continue with fraudulent activities
- conceal a criminal past
- work with children (this may be necessary if the fraudster has been convicted of a criminal offence).

## Identity fraud

Identity fraud is used to describe crimes committed whereby a false or existing identity is used to fraudulently obtain goods or services such as:

- bank accounts
- credit cards
- hire agreements
- loans and mortgages
- state benefits
- mail order goods
- internet purchases
- mobile phone contracts.

## Impersonation of the deceased

This is perhaps the most distressing type of identity-related crime because it affects the family and friends of the deceased. This can be particularly distressing when it involves the identity of a deceased child. A long-standing problem has been that death records are not shared with other organisations. This means that financial organisations have been unable to verify if credit applicants are recorded as deceased and direct mail companies are unaware when deceased people need to be removed from their databases. It is estimated that of the 10 billion pieces of mail annually generated by the direct mail industry, approximately 22 million are regularly sent to deceased people. These mailings can be fraudulently used by criminals to apply for credit cards, loans and mortgages. However, the introduction of a clause to the Police and Justice Act 2006 means that this information can be shared with organisations for the purpose of fraud prevention, detection, investigation and prosecution.

There are also practical and preventative steps you can take to help protect the identity of the deceased. These begin with the death announcement and continue throughout the initial period of bereavement. This can be an extremely traumatic time and protecting the identity of the deceased is not always at the forefront of somebody's mind. However, when a death or funeral is announced try to avoid listing the date of birth, age or address of the deceased. As innocent as these details may appear, they can be used by fraudsters to successfully impersonate the deceased.

It is also important to notify all of the necessary organisations, companies and government departments as soon as possible and that any pension books, allowance books, credit cards or membership cards are either destroyed or returned by recorded delivery. These include:

◆ the deceased's doctor
◆ the deceased's employer
◆ the deceased's solicitor (if applicable)
◆ HM Revenue & Customs
◆ local authorities (council tax, local housing department)
◆ Department for Work & Pensions (DWP)
◆ UK Passport Agency
◆ Driver and Vehicle Licensing Agency (DVLA)
◆ banks and building societies
◆ credit card companies
◆ utility companies (gas, electricity, water, telephone)
◆ Television Licensing
◆ satellite, cable or digital television companies
◆ insurance companies
◆ clubs, associations, season tickets
◆ Royal Mail (for mail redirection).

If any correspondence continues to be received, then it may be necessary to make a formal complaint to the relevant organisation. It is also a good idea to check with Royal Mail that a mail redirection has not been set up on the deceased person's home and to arrange to have their mail redirected to your own address for at least a year. This is particularly important if the property is empty or is for sale because fraudsters have been known to view empty properties with the sole intention of stealing mail. To help avoid this, make sure that all viewings are accompanied and regularly check for mail that may be accidentally delivered.

As an extra security measure, details of the deceased can be registered with the following organisations that specialise in the removal of people from mailing lists:

The Bereavement Register
FREEPOST SEA8240, Sevenoaks, TN13 1YR
Tel: 0870 600 7222
Fax: 0870 400 5644
Email: help@the-bereavement-register.com
www.the-bereavement-register.org.uk

Deceased Preference Service (DPS)
Windhill Manor, Leeds Road, Shipley, BD18 1BP
Tel: 0800 068 4433
www.deceasedpreferenceservice.co.uk

Mail Preference Service (MPS)
FREEPOST 29 LON20771, London, W1E 0ZT
Tel: 0845 703 4599
Fax: 020 7323 4226
Email: mps@dma.org.uk
www.mpsonline.org.uk

Registering with these organisations will help to reduce a vast majority of direct mail but it is also important to ensure that existing correspondence and documents are not inadvertently made available to fraudsters. For example, before disposing of a deceased person's clothes, wallets, handbags or other personal effects, always check that any identity-related items have been removed. Any documents that are no longer required should be shredded before being thrown away because fraudsters can sort through rubbish bags to try to find useable information. For further information regarding destroying and shredding personal information, see page 51, Shredding Your Information.

## Corporate identity crime

It is not only individuals who are susceptible to identity theft. Businesses and business owners can also fall victim to corporate identity crime. As with identity crime, see page 2, the Home Office Steering Committee has developed a series of definitions to differentiate between the various types. The term 'corporate identity crime' is used to describe the three main types of corporate identity-related crimes. These are corporate identity theft, creating a false corporate identity and committing corporate identity fraud.

## Corporate identity theft

This occurs when a genuine business is cloned and its name and credit accounts are used to fraudulently obtain goods, services and money. This is known as corporate identity fraud, see page 8, and is estimated to cost British industry £50 million a year. A company can be cloned by filing fraudulent documents with Companies House to change the registered business address or to appoint directors and thereby create the impression that the fraudster owns the business.

The fraudster can then illegally trade as the genuine company, which means that the genuine company will be liable for all debts incurred by the fraudster. One way to do this is for the fraudster to set up a merchant account in the genuine company's name, accept multiple stolen credit cards and deposit the proceeds in their own bank account. When customers complain that their credit cards have been fraudulently used, the card companies will then charge the genuine company for their losses. Companies House recognises that this is a problem and has introduced a variety of security measures to help companies protect themselves, see page 9.

## Creating a false corporate identity

A false corporate identity is created when fictitious details are used to set up and register a business that does not exist. This can also be achieved by altering the details of a genuine company to create a new business. The overwhelming common dominator in both scenarios is that a false corporate identity is created with the sole purpose of committing fraud. The fraudster can use the details of a fictitious company to order goods with stolen credit cards or credit accounts that appear to be from a genuine company.

## Corporate identity fraud

This is committed when the details of either a genuine business (corporate identity theft) or a fictitious business (false corporate identity) are used to fraudulently obtain goods or services. Fraudsters will go to extraordinary lengths to obtain private and sensitive company information. For example, they will often search through rubbish bins or seek menial employment to discover bank details, steal passes, obtain passwords and acquire other corporate information.

### Companies House

Fraudsters recognise and exploit the fact that Companies House does not have the authority to inspect the contents of documents sent to them for filing. Therefore, it is possible for company details to be changed without their permission or knowledge, so companies are advised to regularly check that their details have not been altered.

To help address this problem, Companies House has taken a proactive approach by introducing a variety of services that allow companies to securely file and electronically check documents:

- WebFiling service
- Software Filing service
- PROOF (PROtectcd Online Filing) service
- Monitor alert system.

To access these services, companies first need to register online with Companies House. During the registration process, stringent security checks are carried out to ensure the applicant is authorised to apply for the service. These checks begin with a security code being sent by email with a further Company Authentication code posted to the company's registered office. Company Authentication codes are unique to each company and are used to verify the identity of a company in the absence of a signature.

*WebFiling service*

This is a safe and secure way for companies to electronically file their statutory information. Companies can save 50% on the cost of filing an annual return and the following documents can be filed online free of charge:

Return of allotment of shares (excluding non-cash) (88 (2))

Notice of increase in nominal capital (with resolution) (123)

Change of accounting reference date (225)

Change in situation or address of registered office (287)

Appointment of director or secretary (288a)

Terminating appointment as director or secretary (288b)

Change of particulars for director or secretary (288c)

Location of register of members (353)

Notice of place for inspection of register of members which is kept in non-legible form, or of any change of that place (353a)

Location of register of debenture holders (190)

Notice of place for inspection of register of holders of debentures which is kept in a non-legible form, or of any change in that place (190a)

Audit Exempt Abbreviated Accounts

Dormant Company Accounts (DCA)

Annual Return (363)

*Software Filing service*

The Software Filing service is primarily aimed at companies who regularly submit statutory documents, such as limited company accounts or annual returns. With this service, these documents can be electronically sent to Companies House by email. These are then automatically authenticated for compliance with the Companies Act prior to being accepted or rejected.

*PROOF (PROtected Online Filing) service*

In addition to their WebFiling and Software Filing services, Companies House has introduced the PROOF service to help companies further reduce the possibility of fraud. To access this service, companies will first need to be a registered WebFiling or Software Filing user. The service works by only allowing companies to electronically file specific forms relating to changes of address and directors' details. Companies House will then reject any paper versions of these forms that claim to come from the company.

The following forms can be submitted under the PROOF service:

Change in situation or address of registered office (287)
Appointment of director or secretary (288a)
Terminating appointment as director or secretary (288b)
Change of particulars for director or secretary (288c)
Annual Return (363)

*Monitor alert system*

As an additional protection service, Companies House has introduced an instant email alerting system, called Monitor. The system allows users to 'monitor' public domain documents filed by themselves, their competitors and business collaborators. As soon as these documents are received, registered and available, users are notified and given the opportunity to order and download this information.

There are also a number of independent companies that offer similar business monitoring services, these include:

Formations House
29 Harley Street, London, W1G 9QR
Tel: 020 7016 2727
Fax: 020 7637 0419
Email: info@formationshouse.com
www.formationshouse.com

Protect My Company
Matthew House, Matthew Street, Dunstable, LU6 1SD
Tel: 0845 400 0777
Email: Admin@ProtectMyCompany.co.uk
www.protectmycompany.co.uk

## HOW YOUR PERSONAL INFORMATION IS USED

After a fraudster has successfully obtained your personal details there are a number of illegal ways that this information can be used. For example, they can either use *some* of your details to create a brand new false identity or they can use *all* of your details to assume your entire identity. Each of these scenarios could potentially leave you liable for any criminal activity committed in your name. However, in reality it is unlikely that you will be prosecuted but clearing your name and restoring credit status can be a lengthy and emotionally draining experience.

A completely new identity may be useful if the fraudster needs to conceal their past. For example, they might have a poor credit history and want to avoid paying their existing debts or they may want to continue breaking the law without arousing suspicion from the police. Other reasons include to work with children, which may be necessary if they need to conceal a criminal past, to drive a vehicle despite being disqualified or to remarry without being divorced first.

When an existing identity is assumed it is generally for the purpose of financial gain. With your personal details and credit rating, fraudsters can obtain goods or services that they have no intention of paying for. They can also apply for financial services such as credit cards, bank accounts, loans, mortgages, mobile phone contracts and state benefits. In addition to this, they can also use your name to apply for passports, driving licences and to register vehicles.

### Funding illegal activities

Identity fraudsters do not conform to a particular profile. They could as easily be working on their own or form part of a larger, highly organised criminal network. These criminal networks commit fraud on a grand scale by acquiring and exploiting multiple identities and are collectively estimated to generate a daily cashflow in the region of £10 million. This is then used to fund other illegal activities such as terrorism, drug smuggling, illegal immigration, people trafficking and money laundering.

### Money laundering

Money laundering is extremely complex and would probably require an entire book to explain it fully. It is particularly linked to identity theft because fraudsters need to legitimately conceal the financial proceeds of their criminal activities. As an overview, money laundering can be described as a three step process:

1. **Placement** – this involves 'placing' money in the financial system, usually as far away from where it originated as possible.

2. **Layering** – moving money through a variety of transactions, in a variety of countries, using a variety of 'shell' companies. 'Shell' companies appear to look legitimate but in fact stand in front of the real company, organisation or individual which profits from the transactions.

3. **Integration** – returning the money to a place where the fraudster can gain access to it. This often involves offshore banking because they have strict privacy laws and minimal regulations, which means that the identity of who owns a company or bank account is almost impossible to determine.

With millions of financial transactions happening every day, tracing the source of laundered money is incredibly difficult. Therefore, law enforcement agencies rely on financial organisations to notify them of any suspicious activity. However, defining exactly what constitutes 'suspicious' is not made clear. In most countries a financial threshold exists, whereby only transactions over this amount need to be reported to the authorities. This has led to the practice of smurfing, which involves processing multiple transactions just below the threshold level.

## TACKLING IDENTITY FRAUD

In recent years, identity fraud has become such a large and growing problem that governments worldwide are constantly finding new ways to address the issue. In the United Kingdom this task has been undertaken by the Home Office which, in 2003, established the Identity Fraud Steering Committee (IFSC) and the Identity Fraud Forum (IFF) which is a joint collaboration between UK financial organisations, government departments and the police. The overreaching objectives of these initiatives include the following.

◆ Identifying new ways to share information between public and private sector organisations.

◆ Reducing fraud involving the impersonation of the deceased.

◆ Accurately recording the cost of identity fraud to the UK economy.

◆ Examining and statistically tracking the effect of identity fraud on victims.

◆ Improving public awareness and providing identity checking training for those in the financial sector.

As part of these initiatives, the Identity Fraud Reduction Work Programme was established to develop and introduce new initiatives to help combat the problem. The programme, which also encompasses the Government's Identity Cards Programme, has successfully launched an identity fraud awareness campaign that includes a comprehensive website, posters and leaflets. Go to Home Office Identity Fraud Steering Committee at www.identity-theft.org.uk

For further information, see page 23, Raising Awareness. In addition to the work of the Home Office, the following new legislation and increased penalties have also been introduced as a deterrent to criminals.

## Criminal Justice Act 2003

Before this Act was introduced, the maximum fine for illegally obtaining a driving licence was only £2,500. However, given the fact that a driving licence is frequently used as a primary source of identity proof, and in view of the vast amount of fraud that can be committed with a counterfeit licence, a £2,500 fine was considered inadequate as a deterrent. The Criminal Justice Act 2003 sought to address the balance by bringing the penalty for illegally obtaining a driving licence in line with the penalty for illegally obtaining a passport. Both of these are now arrestable offences and carry a maximum custodial sentence of two years in prison.

## Identity Cards Act 2006

The Identity Cards Act 2006 received Royal Assent on 30 March 2006 and came into force on 7 June 2006. The main purpose of the Act is to make provision for the introduction of identity cards that the Government intend to introduce as part of the National Identity Scheme. This Act established new criminal offences for possessing, distributing or supplying false identity documents such as passports, immigration papers and driving licences. The Act applies to both UK and foreign documents and also includes genuine documents that have been illegally obtained or have already been issued to somebody else.

## National Identity Scheme

Proving who you are is a necessary and fundamental part of everyday modern life but at present this cannot be done with a single document or a single means of identification. The main problem is that different organisations require different documents to establish identity. In addition, utility bills, statements and other identity confirmation documents can be easily stolen, forged or altered to create a false identity or to steal an existing one.

To address this, the government has taken the first steps towards establishing a National Identity Scheme which is designed to protect identities from being fraudulently used. At the heart of the scheme is the proposed introduction of ID cards to all UK residents over the age of 16. These will provide residents with a simple and secure way to prove who they are with a single means of identification. The scheme was first announced in the Queen's Speech on 17 May 2005 but it will not become fully operational for a number of years.

The scheme will be run by the Identity and Passport Service (IPS) who will work with the Home Office Immigration and Nationality Directorate (IND) and the UK Visa Service to confirm both nationality and identity.

The National Identity Scheme will comprise four main components:

1. enrolment
2. National Identity Register (NIR)
3. identity cards
4. identity verification service.

*Enrolment*

The first stage of enrolment is registering your identity. This is a two-stage process that involves creating a biographical footprint and recording your biometric data. A biographical footprint is simply a record of your name, address and date of birth. When you apply for an ID card these details are then cross-referenced against other identity verification databases such as National Insurance, DVLA and the electoral roll.

Registering your biometric data is an essential part of the enrolment process and involves creating high quality digital images of your face, irises and fingerprints. This unique data is then permanently linked to your biographical information to definitively prove who you are. To make enrolment accessible to as many people as possible, a number of local enrolment centres will be created with additional mobile centres being used for rural areas.

*National Identity Register (NIR)*

The National Identity Register will only be used to collate and store identity-related biographical and biometric information. Additional personal data such as medical records, tax details, benefits information and other government records will not be included in the register. However, the register can be accessed by relevant organisations to confirm if the information contained within their own systems agrees with those in the register.

*Identity cards*

The first identity cards are not due to be issued until 2009, when they will initially be available with adult passports and renewals. Until 1 January 2010 you will have the option to decline an ID card when you receive a passport but your details will still be entered into the National Identity Register. Stand-alone ID cards will become available at a later date for people who do not want or need a passport. The cards will be similar in size to a credit card and will contain:

- your name
- an image of your face
- your unique Identity Registration Number (IRN)
- an electronic chip with basic identity information
- a Personal Identification Number (PIN), that can be set in the same way as a credit card PIN.

*Identity verification service*

With your consent, approved organisations will be able to use this service to confirm your identity. There are many different situations when this may be useful, for example when opening a bank account, registering with a doctor, applying for a job or hiring a car. The service will offer a variety of identity-checking options that range from a basic search to prove your age to whether you have a criminal record.

## Fraud Act 2006

The Fraud Act 2006 received Royal Assent on 8 November 2006 and came into force on 15 January 2007. The purpose of the Act was to simplify and replace the existing common law offence of 'conspiracy to defraud' with a new, statutory offence for fraud. This new offence defines three separate ways of committing fraud.

1. **By false representation** – i.e. creating or selling counterfeit goods, dishonestly using a credit card, phishing over the internet or committing corporate identity theft.

2. **By failing to disclose information** – i.e. providing false or inaccurate details on insurance proposals or solicitors not sharing important information with their clients.

3. **By abuse of position** – i.e. employees who steal from their employers or someone who acts for personal gain against the best interests of clients or the company.

In each of these cases, fraud can be proven if the person has acted dishonestly with the intention of making a gain for either themselves or someone else or if they have inflicted a loss or potential loss on someone else. This means that identity-related frauds that were previously difficult to prosecute, such as those involving counterfeit goods, credit cards or phishing can now be more easily prosecuted.

The Act has also created new fraud offences:

◆ **Obtaining services dishonestly**
   This includes illegally downloading music, software or movies, fraudulently using false credit card details or receiving satellite television with no intention of paying.

◆ **Possessing, making and supplying articles for use in frauds**
   These include machines that can be used to clone credit

cards, illegally view satellite television or cause electricity meters to give false readings. This could also include lists of credit card details, computer programs to create credit card numbers or templates for phishing and scam letters.

◆ **Participating in a fraudulent business**
This includes selling counterfeit goods, being a bogus charity collector, knowingly defrauding customers and suppliers or using the business as a barrier between the fraudster and the victims. This offence also extends to sole traders, trusts and partnerships.

## Working together

Identity-related crimes span a variety of different industries and therefore it has been necessary for companies and organisations to work together in an attempt to combat the problem. For example, the Identity and Passport Service (IPS) and the Driver Vehicle Licensing Authority (DVLA) work jointly to ensure that the most stringent and highest levels of identity checking are constantly applied before passports and driving licences are issued. The IPS also shares its database of lost and stolen passports with international police forces and border authorities through Interpol.

The IPS was established on 1 April 2006 as an Executive Agency of the Home Office to work closely with the Border and Immigration Agency, the Foreign and Commonwealth Office and UK Visas. One of its primary objectives is to develop and introduce common working practices between organisations regarding the way that identity-related information is exchanged and managed.

When the National Identity Scheme is introduced, the IPS will be responsible for issuing ID cards for British and Irish nationals living in the UK. It will also link the scheme to foreign nationals living in the UK by issuing biometric immigration documents.

In addition, the Home Office, DVLA and UK Passport Service (UKPS) have worked alongside the Finance and Leasing Association (FLA), APACS and the Credit Industry Fraud Advisory Scheme (CIFAS) to produce *Identity Fraud – The UK Manual*. This manual is specifically designed to help organisations identify counterfeit passports and driving licences by highlighting the existing and changing security features of genuine documents.

Another example of the way that identity information is shared can be seen through the introduction of a clause to the Police and Justice Act 2006 regarding the deceased. This clause means that death registration information can be shared with organisations for the purpose of fraud prevention, detection, investigation and prosecution. With this information becoming available it is anticipated that fraud involving the impersonation of the deceased will be dramatically reduced and eventually completely eradicated, see page 4, Impersonation of the Deceased.

## FRAUD PREVENTION MEASURES

With identity-related crime continuing to increase, a variety of fraud prevention measures have already been introduced with many more being developed. These include the introduction of the following.

- Chip and PIN technology which has resulted in a significant reduction in credit card fraud.

- A Dedicated Cheque and Plastic Crime Unit (DCPCU) to tackle plastic and cheque fraud.

- Secure payment systems such as MasterCard Secure Code and Verified by Visa for online transactions.

- The Industry Hot Card File which allows retailers to check if a card is being fraudulently used.

- A verification system to confirm if the cardholder address and card security code system is correct when accepting internet and telephone orders.

- Intelligent fraud detection systems that are designed to identify fraud by checking for unusual spending patterns.

### Raising awareness

At the heart of the fight against identity-related crime is the necessity to raise awareness of the problem. The Home Office Identity Fraud Steering Committee has developed a very informative website which is an excellent place to start. Go to Home Office Identity Fraud Steering Committee at www.identity-theft.org.uk

In addition to providing general identity theft-related information, the Home Office has also produced an *Identity Theft – Don't Become a Victim* leaflet together with a series of posters. These have been distributed to a wide range of places including Citizens Advice offices, police stations, public libraries, passport offices, the DVLA, doctors' surgeries and victim support schemes.

They are also available to download from the website, see page 23.

## National Identity Fraud Prevention Week

Identity fraud has become such a major concern that an annual awareness campaign has been launched to help people protect themselves by providing practical help and advice. The National Identity Fraud Prevention Week takes place every October and has been put in place by a variety of organisations including the Metropolitan Police (and other regional police forces), CIFAS, Royal Mail, Federation of Small Businesses (FSB), Callcredit, Experian, Equifax, DVLA, Identity and Passport Service, British Bankers' Association (BBA), HM Revenue & Customs, APACS, SOCA, City of London Police, the FSA and Fellowes. For further information visit the campaign's dedicated website at www.stop-idfraud.co.uk

## Identity fraud related websites

Owing to the growth of identity related crime, a number of websites have been launched to provide help, advice and guidance about identity theft and protecting yourself from its associated consequences. These include:

Anti-Phishing Working Group – www.antiphishing.org
Cross-industry global group supporting those tackling phishing and pharming by providing advice on anti-phishing controls and information on current trends.

APACS – www.apacs.org.uk
Association for Payment Clearing Services (APACS), is the UK trade association for the banking industry that provides a forum for its members to come together on

non-competitive issues relating to the payments industry. They also work with police, retailers, cardholders and organisations to fight payment card fraud.

Bank Safe Online – www.banksafeonline.org.uk
Bank Safe Online is run by APACS on behalf of its member banks to help online banking customers stay safe online.

Card Watch – www.cardwatch.org.uk
Card Watch raises awareness about all types of plastic card fraud in the UK and provides information to prevent fraudulent use of credit cards, debit cards, cheque guarantee cards and charge cards.

Consumer Direct – www.consumerdirect.gov.uk
A government-funded telephone and online advice service operated by the Office of Fair Trading (OFT) providing clear, practical advice on a wide range of consumer issues. The advice is free and you can call 0845 404 0506 as many times as you need to.

Dedicated Cheque and Plastic Crime Unit (DCPCU) – www.dcpcu.org.uk
The DCPCU is sponsored by APACS on behalf of the banking industry, it comprises a group of specialist police officers and civilian staff to tackle the organised gangs responsible for much of the UK's card and cheque fraud.

Get Safe Online – www.getsafeonline.org.uk
Protect yourself from identity thieves, viruses, phishing and other internet threats with expert advice from the British Government, the Serious and Organised Crime

Agency and industry specialists who will help you guard against online dangers.

Fraud Watch International – www.fraudwatchinternational.com
Combines anti-phishing education, monitoring and detection services and preventative software solutions for consumers and corporate clients.

ID Theft Protect – www.id-protect.co.uk
Provides guidance and a comprehensive step-by-step programme designed to protect you from identity fraud.

Microsoft Security At Home – www.microsoft.com/security/protect
Useful help and advice to protect your computer, yourself and your family from online threats and inappropriate content and contact.

Miller Smiles – www.millersmiles.co.uk
A large archive of spoof email and phishing scams.

Serious Organised Crime Agency (SOCA) – www.soca.gov.uk
Non-geographic police unit responsible for undertaking pro-active operations against serious and organised crime.

Spamfo – www.spamfo.co.uk
Organised collection of news, reviews and links about unsolicited bulk email (spam).

Shop Safe Online – www.shopsafeonline.org.uk
Provides information about registering and using MasterCard SecureCode and Verified by Visa.

Shopsafe UK – www.shopsafe.co.uk
A UK online shopping directory listing secure UK online shops so you can shop on the internet with confidence. The site also includes special offers, gift ideas and safe shopping advice.

Stay Safe Online – www.staysafeonline.info
Provides free and non-technical cyber security and safety resources to the public, so that consumers, small businesses and educators have the know-how to avoid cyber crime.

## VICTIMS' STORIES

### Impersonation of the deceased fraud

After Jack's father died, his bank accounts were closed, credit cards were cancelled and his mail was redirected. However, within a short while Jack started to receive letters from credit card companies, debt collection agencies and department stores claiming that his father had failed to make repayments on credit and store cards that he had taken out. Jack contacted each company but was disappointed to receive a mixed response ranging from a lack of interest to disbelief of who he was. Jack's father had always paid his bills on time and had never been in debt so Jack was devastated that his father's reputation was being tarnished. After two years of continual correspondence, the situation was eventually resolved but not before more credit cards and store cards were taken out.

### Corporate identity fraud

When ABC Computing registered with a risk-monitoring service they knew they would be notified when another business with the same name filed any papers at Companies

House. When this happened they checked with Companies House and discovered that a change of address had been filed against their own business. Before the unauthorised changes could be restored, ABC Computing had to apply to the High Court for a Court Order which took a great deal of time and money to sort out. This had a detrimental effect on the business because during this period, marketing campaigns and product launches had to be cancelled. In addition to notifying their bank, they also had to inform every customer and supplier to ensure their business remained intact.

Since this unfortunate incident, ABC Computing has signed up for the PROOF (PROtected Online Filing) service provided by Companies House. This is a password protected service that only permits nominated company owners to make changes online. By signing up to this service, Companies House will now reject any paper documents from ABC Computing which means that their corporate identity can be fully protected.

$$\left(\,2\,\right)$$

# Protecting Your Identity

Your personal information is an extremely valuable commodity and criminals will go to extraordinary lengths to steal it from you. Therefore, it is important to protect and safeguard your identity at all times. This can sometimes be difficult because there are legitimate occasions when it will be necessary to disclose personal information, for example, when applying for credit, joining a club, hiring a vehicle or opening an account. The real difficulty comes when you are unexpectedly asked for information in circumstances that may appear genuine but which have been carefully orchestrated by fraudsters. This chapter will look at how your identity can be stolen and will offer practical help and advice about how to reduce the risk of this happening.

## KEEPING YOUR IDENTITY SAFE
In addition to directly stealing your personal information, criminals also use various indirect methods to steal your details through email, telephone, fax or canvassing. In recent years, the advancement of home computers has made it possible to create official-looking documents, headed notepaper and emails that can easily pass as genuine to the casual observer. Unsolicited emails or spam, as it is more commonly known, is an efficient way

to target millions of potential victims at next to no cost. This is covered in more detail in Chapter 3, see page 90, Spam.

Unsolicited letters and faxes are often used to advise you that you have either won a lottery or are about to inherit some money. You will then be asked to provide your bank details to enable the funds to be transferred, which of course do not exist. Instead, this information will be used by criminals to clear your bank account. Telephone canvassing is a popular marketing method that companies use to retain existing customers and generate new business. In order to ensure that they are speaking to the right person, they will often ask the customer a series of security questions. In most cases, this is a perfectly legitimate process that is designed to protect both the customer and the company.

**Giving out your personal information**
Fraudsters employ similar techniques to get your personal information by claiming to be from your bank or credit card company. A common scam is to persuade you to confirm your account number, password or PIN as a security measure when in fact the caller never has this information in the first place. Remember that genuine companies will never request your details in this way, so always be extra vigilant when dealing with these types of calls. If you have any suspicions about the caller then either end the call immediately or insist on verifying the caller's identity. Genuine callers will not object to this and they will probably welcome your security concerns. This can be done by politely offering to call them back through

the main company switchboard. Never return a call to a direct line because this will not necessarily confirm where they are calling from.

When giving out your personal information, it is essential to exercise extreme caution. Always think about who is asking for your information, why they need it and whether they are genuine. Even the most friendly or official-looking people may not always be what they seem, so if you have any doubts about who you are dealing with then the golden rule is to never give out your information.

### Reducing unsolicited communication

Unsolicited telephone calls, mail, faxes and emails can be obtrusive, annoying and time consuming to deal with. They also mean that your personal details are in a number of sales and marketing databases, which are often sold on to other companies. Fortunately, by registering with the Telephone Preference Service (TPS), Mail Preference Service (MPS), Fax Preference Service (FPS) and the Email Preference Service (eMPS) you can greatly reduce these types of unsolicited communication. After registering, you will still receive information from organisations with whom you have a continuing relationship such as mail order companies or charities. The only exception would be if you have specifically asked them not to contact you in this way.

Registration to these services is completely free, so if you are ever asked for payment to register then refuse and immediately notify the relevant preference service because this will be a scam. To register with the TPS, MPS, FPS or eMPS contact:

Telephone Preference Service (TPS)
3rd Floor, DMA House, 70 Margaret Street, London,
W1W 8SS
TPS Registration Line: 0845 070 0707
Tel: 0845 703 4599
Fax: 020 7323 4226
Email: tps@dma.org.uk
www.tpsonline.org.uk

Mail Preference Service (MPS)
FREEPOST 29 LON20771, London, W1E 0ZT
MPS Registration Line: 0845 703 4599
Tel: 0845 703 4599
Fax: 020 7323 4226
Email: mps@dma.org.uk
www.mpsonline.org.uk

Fax Preference Service (FPS)
3rd Floor, DMA House, 70 Margaret Street, London,
W1W 8SS
FPS Registration Line: 0845 070 0702
Tel: 0845 703 4599
Fax: 020 7323 4226
Email: fps@dma.org.uk
www.fpsonline.org.uk

Email Preference Service (eMPS)
www.dmachoice.org/EMPS/
This global service is managed by the Direct Marketing
Association in America, which allows you to register your
email address so you do not receive unsolicited sales and
marketing email messages from companies or organisations who use eMPS to clean their lists.

Before registering with any of these services it is worth considering that you will no longer receive information that may have been of interest to you. For example, some companies and organisations use these methods to advertise special offers or new products and services. Charities also use these methods to raise awareness and generate support. As an alternative you could contact specific organisations that you do not want to receive information from and ask for your details to be removed from their lists. However, from an identity-related perspective it is highly advisable to register with each of these services.

### Social networking

Social networking is a relatively new and exciting way to search, find and stay in touch with friends, family and work colleagues. Popular sites such as Bebo, Facebook, Friends Reunited, MySpace, and Saga Zone allow users to create and upload personal profiles but, unfortunately, not everybody is searching for people they know. Criminals are also using these sites to collect personal data that they can fraudulently use.

Personal profiles will often contain seemingly innocent information such as date of birth, place of birth, mother's maiden name, schools attended, pet's name, previous and current addresses, telephone numbers and email addresses. However, this information is highly sought after by criminals because it is often used as passwords or by organisations to confirm an identity. Social networking is an extremely popular online activity but you need to think carefully about the information you are making available because it can be used by criminals to apply for credit, steal your identity or apply for benefits. Fortunately, there are a variety of precautionary measures that can be taken to protect yourself and your identity.

◆ **Do not publish any common verification details**
These include your date of birth, place of birth, mother's maiden name, schools attended, pet's name, address, telephone numbers or email address.

◆ **Use the privacy settings**
Most websites have privacy filters that allow you to control who can see your profile, who can find you and how much information you want them to see.

◆ **Choose who you accept as a friend**
Do not automatically accept everyone as a friend and provide them with full access to your profile. Only accept people that you know and consider limiting access to those people that you do not know well.

◆ **Do not publish your precise holiday arrangements**
This information could be used by burglars to find empty properties which could also possibly invalidate any insurance claim.

◆ **Be careful about the information you publish**
These websites are often searched by potential and current employers so be careful about what information you want to become publicly available. Never publish anything that could incriminate you or hinder your employment prospects.

## USING CREDIT AND DEBIT CARDS SAFELY

Credit and debit cards have become a large part of our everyday lives and are an easy way to pay for goods or services. Unfortunately, they have also become a target for fraud which is estimated to cost the UK economy around £1 million a day. New initiatives such as Chip and PIN are helping to reduce this figure but users need to help themselves. Fortunately, there a number of preventive measures that can be adopted to use your cards safely:

◆ **Keep your account number, password and PIN secure**
Do not carry your password or PIN with you or disclose the number to anyone, even if they claim to be from your card company or the police. Your card company will never ask for your full password or PIN so always be wary if you are asked for this information. If you are unsure whether the caller is genuine, then offer to call them back on a recognised number. Never call back on a direct line because you can not guarantee exactly where they are.

◆ **Never let your card out of your sight**
This particularly applies when using your card in a retail outlet such as a shop, restaurant or petrol station. Ask for the card terminal to be brought to you or accompany the member of staff to the till. Fraudsters can swipe your card through a skimming machine, make a note of your security number and create a clone from the card's magnetic strip, see page 40, Counterfeit and Cloned Card Fraud (Skimming).

◆ **Shield your PIN from prying eyes**
When using your card in a public place always shield

the keypad with your free hand. This will prevent anyone from 'shoulder surfing' or watching security cameras to get your PIN, see page 42, Cash machine fraud.

◆ **Only buy from recognised websites**
When shopping online only buy from recognised websites that have a landline and a full postal address. Never buy from a website that uses a mobile number or a PO Box address because it may be difficult to resolve any problems that may arise. Look out for websites that promote MasterCard SecureCode or Verified by Visa which offer enhanced security features when buying over the internet, see page 126, Shopping Online.

◆ **Regularly check your bank and card statements**
It is important to carefully check your bank and card statements and immediately query any transactions that you do not recognise. If you have internet banking then this can be done on a regular basis without having to wait for your monthly statement.

◆ **Always shred card statements and receipts**
Always use a cross-cut (confetti) shredder to dispose of unwanted bank or card statements and receipts. Fraudsters have been known to search through rubbish bins for information to fraudulently use, see page 51, Shredding Your Information.

◆ **Never carry more cards than you need**
Before you leave home, think about where you are going and which cards you will need. There is no point in carrying more cards than are necessary because this

will only increase the chance of cards becoming lost or stolen.

## Protecting your cards

If your credit or debit cards are lost or stolen then it is important to cancel them immediately by notifying your card providers. This will prevent thieves, criminals and fraudsters from using your cards to obtain goods or services illegally. To ease this process it is advisable to create a list of your card numbers and keep this together with a list of their respective emergency telephone numbers. Alternatively, your cards can be registered with a card protection company. Depending on which company you use and which level of protection you buy, insurance policies range from between £12 and £30 per year. Some policies can be extended to include other family members and most companies will offer a discount if you sign up for more than a year at a time, so it is worth shopping around.

## Card insurance policy benefits

As with any type of insurance, no two companies are the same and no two policies will provide the same level of protection or offer the same range of benefits. Therefore, it is essential to carefully consider exactly what each company is offering before signing up to any policy. Card insurance policies will include a variation of the following benefits.

- ◆ Card cancellation and replacement service for all of your registered cards.

- ◆ Cover against the fraudulent use of your cards if they are lost or stolen.

- Change of address service to notify card providers when you move.

- Passport and driving licence replacement service.

- Cash replacement if money is lost or stolen with your cards.

- Emergency cash advance for travel tickets or hotel costs if you become stranded abroad.

- Communication costs for notifying the police or insurers about lost or stolen cards, tickets or property.

- Security labels for luggage and keys to encourage the finder to return your lost property.

- Replacement cover if your wallet, briefcase, handbag, purse etc is stolen with your cards.

There are many different card protection companies to choose from but which type of policy is best for you will depend on your personal needs. Further information can be obtained from:

Card Protection Plan (CPP)
Holgate Park, York, YO26 4GA
Tel: 0870 608 1529
www.cpp.co.uk

Sentinel Card Protection
FREEPOST PT391, Portsmouth, PO3 5BR
Tel: 0800 414 717
www.sentinelcardprotection.com

In addition to these, banks and other financial institutions will either offer their own range of card insurance policies or have their own preferred card protection supplier. So if you are considering card protection insurance it is worth contacting these organisations in the first instance, because they will sometimes offer discounts to existing customers.

## TYPES OF CARD FRAUD

According to APACS card fraud is estimated to cost the UK economy approximately £430 million per year. Unfortunately, this huge figure is not the result of one particular type of fraud that can be easily identified, rectified and reduced. Instead, the figure comprises a variety of different types of card fraud which include:

- lost or stolen card fraud
- card identity theft
- card-not-present (CNP) fraud
- counterfeit and cloned card fraud (skimming)
- postal interception fraud
- cashpoint fraud.

### Lost or stolen card fraud

This occurs when a criminal poses as you to obtain goods and services with your lost or stolen card. The majority of this fraud happens before the loss has been reported so it is important to immediately notify card companies as soon as you realise that your card has been lost or stolen. For further information, see page 35, Using Credit and Debit Cards Safely.

## Card identity theft

With just a few of your utility bills or bank statements it is possible for criminals to assemble enough information to apply successfully for new credit cards or take over your existing accounts. Therefore, it is important to always shred personal documents that you no longer need. Criminals will use whatever they can find to convince financial organisations that they are you. They can also arrange for funds to be taken from your account, for your address to be changed and for new cheque books and cards to be sent to the new address.

## Card-not-present (CNP) fraud

As the name suggests, this happens when a card is not required at the point of sale to complete a purchase, such as through mail order, over the telephone or online. The problem for companies is that without physically seeing the card, it is very difficult to confirm if the card and the customer are genuine. This means that once a criminal has stolen your card, copied your number or found your old receipts, they can then attempt to use your card fraudulently. Since the introduction of chip and PIN, this has become the most common type of card fraud in the UK.

## Counterfeit and cloned card fraud (skimming)

Counterfeit and cloned cards are produced by electronically copying (skimming) data from your genuine card onto a fake blank card without your knowledge. This involves swiping the magnetic strip of your card through an electronic device which captures your account information. Skimming can occur whenever your card is used to pay for goods or services so always ensure that your card is kept in full view at all times. A common scam is for the shop assistant to accidentally drop your card and then quickly swipe it before you realise what has happened. Skimming devices can also be fitted to cash machines to get your details, see page 42, Cash Machine Fraud.

Skimming has been around for quite a while, but Chip and PIN technology has severely limited the number of places where a criminal can attempt to use a counterfeit card. Only outlets and overseas cash machines that have not yet upgraded to Chip and PIN can be targeted by criminals with counterfeit cards. However, a criminal must also have your PIN number to use a counterfeit card in an overseas cash machine. Counterfeit cards are essentially a duplicate of your original card and therefore you will probably be unaware that your card has been skimmed until your statement arrives.

### Postal interception card fraud

This happens when your new card is stolen in transit before the card company has been able to deliver it to you. People who live in properties with shared letterboxes such as in flats or student accommodation and people who have failed to have their post redirected after moving are particularly vulnerable to having their post stolen. If you suspect that your post has been lost, stolen or tampered with, then contact Royal Mail Customer Care on 0845 774 0740. For further information, see page 46, Securing Your Post.

## Cash machine fraud

There are a number of ways that cash machines can be used to steal from you so it is important to exercise caution when using them. Pickpockets often operate near cash machines so always put your cash and card safely away before leaving the machine. Thieves have been known to snatch money straight from the machine or from your hand. Since the introduction of Chip and PIN technology, credit and debit cards are not as useful to criminals as they used to be without your PIN. But when criminals have both your card and your PIN they can simply use the nearest cash machine to access your money, so never keep them together in case they become lost or stolen. This is why it is important to memorise your PIN and shred the notification slip as soon as possible. To get your PIN, criminals will often use a technique called 'shoulder surfing'.

### Shoulder surfing

This happens when criminals look over your shoulder as you enter your PIN at a cash machine or card terminal in a shop, restaurant or garage. They will then attempt to steal and use your card before you even notice it is missing. Therefore, it is important to protect your PIN by never telling anyone the number or letting anyone see you enter the number. You can do this by covering the keypad with your free hand and also by positioning yourself to shield the keypad from potential onlookers. Criminals who shoulder surf are very discreet so you may not even notice that you are being watched.

Alternatively, criminals can use card trapping or skimming techniques to obtain your card by tampering with cash machines. Before inserting your card into a cash machine, always check for tampering by running your thumb across the card slot. If you can feel any protrusions then the machine may have been tampered with so do not use it. Instead, walk away and immediately contact the police or the bank. Criminals will usually only target external machines so, whenever possible, always use a cash machine inside the bank.

### Card trapping

This involves fixing a thin plastic or metal sleeve into the card slot of a cash machine that will trap your card so you think the machine has stopped working or retained your card. The criminal will then watch as you enter your PIN and may even helpfully encourage you to re-enter the number to try to get your card back – which will obviously not work. After you have left the machine, the criminal will then retrieve your card and use your PIN to steal your money. A more sophisticated variation of card trapping involves recording your PIN by attaching a small pinhole camera or a fake keypad to the machine.

### Skimming

This is an electronic device that is discreetly fitted to the entrance of the card slot to read and record the information on the magnetic strip as the card enters the machine. This technique does not involve retaining the card because the information is used to create a duplicate (cloned) card by copying the data onto a blank magnetic strip. The cloned card can then be used as normal to shop or withdraw money from your account. Some skimming machines involve fitting an entire false fascia to the outside of the machine that appears completely genuine.

If you notice that a card trapping or skimming device has been attached to the machine, do not attempt to remove it. Some of these devices can be very expensive and criminals may use violence to protect them. Instead, walk away and immediately contact the police or the bank. Further information about card fraud prevention can be obtained from the following organisations.

APACS – www.apacs.org.uk
The Association for Payment Clearing Services (APACS) works with the police, retailers, cardholders and organisations to fight payment card fraud.

Card Watch – www.cardwatch.org.uk
Card Watch raises awareness about all types of plastic card fraud in the UK and provides information to prevent fraudulent use of credit cards, debit cards, cheque guarantee cards and charge cards.

DCPCU – www.dcpcu.org.uk
The Dedicated Cheque and Plastic Crime Unit (DCPCU) is sponsored by APACS on behalf of the banking industry. It comprises a group of specialist police officers and civilian staff to tackle the organised gangs responsible for much of the UK's card and cheque fraud.

Shop Safe Online – www.shopsafeonline.org.uk
Provides information about registering and using Master CardSecureCode and Verified by Visa.

## KEEPING YOUR PERSONAL DOCUMENTS SECURE

Personal documents are just as valuable to thieves as any of your other possessions such as electrical goods, jewellery, paintings and antiques. Although your possessions have an immediate resale value, there is also a growing market for personal documents that can either be sold to identity fraudsters or retained by the thief for their own use. The types of documents that are particularly attractive to thieves and fraudsters include:

- passports
- birth certificates
- driving licences
- marriage certificates
- vehicle registration documents
- insurance documents
- utility bills
- share certificates.

A fraudster only requires a small selection of these to assume your identity and steal from you so it is very important to ensure that your documents are always kept safe and secure. There are also a number of preventive measures you can employ to help safeguard your documents, these include the following.

### Storing documents at home

Any documents that are kept at home should be stored in either a secure cabinet, a lockable drawer, a home safe or ideally a combination of all three. Always avoid keeping your documents in one place because if a thief finds them, then they will have instant access to whatever they need. Instead, use a variety of secure locations and remember the more difficult you make it for thieves to find your documents then the less likely they are to steal them.

## Using a bank

For valuable documents with a high financial or senti-
mental value such as title deeds, share certificates, or
irreplaceable family documents, consider using a bank or
solicitor to secure them on your behalf. Unless you are a
premium customer, then most banks will charge a fee for
this service but this is money well spent against the
possibility of having them stolen.

## Carrying personal documents

Whenever you carry personal documents there is always a
risk that they will become lost or stolen. You can reduce
this risk by only carrying documents that are absolutely
necessary so before you leave home, think about where
you are going and what you really need. For example, you
will probably have more than one credit card but do you
need to take all of them with you. One card is useful for
emergency purposes but any others should be left safely at
home. From a security perspective, you should also avoid
carrying your PIN number with your cards.

Similarly your driving licence, vehicle registration and
insurance documents are useful if you are stopped by the
police whilst driving but they are not always needed and
they should certainly never be left in an unattended
vehicle. Other important documents to avoid carrying are
your passport and birth certificate which should only be
taken out of the house when it is absolutely necessary.

## Securing your post

The majority of personal documents are sent through the
post and although some are sent by recorded or registered
delivery this is not always the case. Despite the problems

of card fraud it is surprising that banks and card companies still only use standard mail to send out card and cheque books. It is possible that your post can be intercepted or stolen and this is most likely to happen if you live in a shared house or a flat with a communal letterbox. To reduce this risk, arrange to collect these from your bank or try to collect your mail as soon after it has been delivered as possible. Obviously this can be difficult if you are regularly out when the postman calls so it may be worth installing a separate lockable letterbox to safely secure your post. These are relatively inexpensive but are worth every penny for the peace of mind they provide.

When you are away from home for an extended period or if you want to protect the security of your post, arrange to have it held at your local delivery office until you return or until it can be collected. Royal Mail offers a Mail Collect service, a Keepsafe service and they can also provide a rented PO Box.

### Mail Collect service

This is a free service that allows you to collect your post from your local delivery office. To sign up for this, simply complete a Mail Collect application form (P6266) and return it to your local delivery office together with your proof of identification. For further information, contact the Royal Mail Sales Centre on 0845 795 0950.

### Keepsafe service

This service can be used to hold your mail for up to two months and then deliver it upon your return. This costs from £5.70 for two weeks and will avoid returning to a pile of unopened mail on your doorstep. For further information contact the Royal Mail Keepsafe Team on 0845 777 7888.

## PO Boxes

PO Boxes enable your mail to be safely delivered to a rented box at your local delivery office for collection at a time convenient to you. These cost £57.85 for a year or £46.95 for six months. Further information can be obtained from the Royal Mail Sales Centre on 0845 795 0950.

Alternatively, ask someone who you trust to deal with your post in your absence. However, if you suspect that your post has been tampered with, has been stolen or has gone missing, then contact Royal Mail Customer Care on 0845 774 0740.

## DESTROYING YOUR PERSONAL INFORMATION

Your name and address is relatively easy for fraudsters to get and is often the starting point for fraud. Fraudsters only need a few of your personal details to steal your identity so it is essential that any documents with your name, address, signature, account numbers or other seemingly innocent information are completely destroyed before being thrown away. Some of these documents include:

- bank and credit card statements
- receipts and invoices
- utility bills

- pre-completed application forms
- pre-approved credit card application forms
- cheque book counterfoils
- credit or debit card transaction receipts
- National Insurance letters
- payslips
- working tax forms
- Inland Revenue tax reminders
- car tax reminders
- letterheads
- direct mail letters (junk mail)
- subscription renewal notices
- expired driving licences or passports
- magazine mailing labels
- appointment letters and reminders (doctor, dentist, hospital)
- insurance forms
- expired credit, debit and store cards
- expired membership or insurance cards
- any other documents that contain personal details.

Any of these documents can be used by fraudsters but despite warnings to the contrary, many people throw these away without realising their worth to criminals. This has resulted in everyday rubbish becoming an unlikely target for theft. In fact some organised gangs have been known to pay people to steal or search through rubbish bags, which is more commonly known as 'bin raiding'.

### Bin raiding

Rubbish is an easy target for thieves because it is usually left outside, which not only makes it easily accessible but you may also be unaware that it has been raided or stolen. Your rubbish can potentially contain all that a fraudster needs to steal from you so it is important to carefully consider what information you are throwing away. Junk mail is one of the most common pieces of rubbish to be thrown away and will often be unopened. At the very least, this will contain your name and address but if you have previously ordered from a catalogue, donated to charity or subscribed to a magazine, organisation or club, then your mail can also contain all kinds of other information that will be very useful to a criminal.

For example, unopened letters could contain your account number or a change of address card. Criminals can use this information to contact the sender and change your address which means that your name and credit rating will move to theirs. Some companies carry out extensive checks to prevent this from happening but not all companies are as thorough. Unless you know exactly when your bank or credit card statements are due you may not even realise that your address has been changed. For peace of mind, it is worth keeping a record of when regular and important correspondence is expected and immediately contact the company concerned if your mail is late. You can also check with Royal Mail Customer Care on 0845 774 0740 if you have any concerns about your mail.

Credit card applications are another useful source of information because they are often partially completed to encourage you to apply. Criminals can use these to apply for a credit card, have it sent to their address and then apply for other cards and loans using your name and credit rating. Payslips are also useful because they can be scanned, altered and used to apply for a mortgage. Your date of birth is a little more difficult to get but is not impossible because it will often be written on medical-related letters such as appointment reminders. Some people also use their date of birth as a PIN number so this can be very useful to criminals.

Since the introduction of Chip and PIN (see page 39, Types of Card Fraud) your signature is not as valuable to criminals as it once was, but banks and other companies will sometimes require written confirmation before changing your address. Your signature can also be difficult to get but simple oversights such as putting all the pieces of a cut-up credit card into the same bin can be disastrous because they can easily be reassembled. In fact, any personal information that has been ripped up can be put back together so it's very important to shred any documents that could be useful to a criminal.

## SHREDDING YOUR INFORMATION

One of the best ways to ensure that your important documents are completely destroyed is to use a shredder. These can be bought from most high street stationers and office supply companies and vary according to their features, intended use and level of security. In addition to paper, shredders are capable of shredding a variety of other items such as floppy discs, compact discs, DVDs, credit cards, staples and paperclips. There are two different types of shredder:

- strip-cut shredder
- cross-cut shredder.

## Strip-cut shredders

These cut paper into long thin strips that vary in width from 1.9mm to 10.5mm. From a security point of view they are less effective than cross-cut shredders because with a little glue and a lot of patience, a document can be restored to its original state. Strip-cut shredders are suitable for everyday non-sensitive documents but for documents containing any personal information such as bank details, utility bills or passwords then a cross-cut shredder is highly recommended.

## Cross-cut shredders

Cross-cut shredders cut paper into tiny pieces (particles) that vary in size from 0.78mm × 11mm to 10.5mm × 80mm. In addition to increased security, the particles also compact under their own weight, which means that the waste box will require emptying less often.

## Choosing a shredder

The type of shredder best suited to your needs will depend on how often the machine is to be used and which level of security you require. As with most business machines, shredders are manufactured for different markets.

- **Home shredders** – suitable for light use of up to 20 sheets a day.

- **Home office shredders** – suitable for light to medium use of up to 50 sheets a day.

- **Office shredders** – suitable for medium use of up to 100 sheets a day.

- **Business shredders** – suitable for heavy, continuous use.

### Security levels

Shredders are assigned a security level in accordance with the Deutsche Industrial Norm (DIN) which ranges from DIN 1 (low security) to DIN 5 (high security). These security levels relate to how small the machine will shred the paper. DIN security levels have been specifically designed to standardise shredder production and help you make an informed choice when buying a shredder.

- **DIN 1 – low security (general documents)**
  This is suitable for general paperwork that does not contain any personal information. A strip-cut shredder will produce single strips that vary from 10.5mm to 11.8mm wide and a cross-cut shredder will create pieces ranging from 10.5mm × 40mm to 10.5mm × 80mm.

- **DIN 2 – low to medium security (internal documents)**
  A strip-cut shredder will produce single strips that vary from 3.9mm to 5.8mm wide and a cross-cut shredder will create pieces ranging from 7.5mm × 40mm to 7.5mm × 80mm. This level of security is suitable for home use and internal office documents such as computer printouts, personal notes and poor quality photocopies.

- **DIN 3 – medium security (confidential documents)**
  This is recommended for confidential business documents such as financial papers, marketing plans or

personnel files. Strip-cut shredders will cut extremely narrow strips of up 1.9mm wide and cross-cut shredders will create small particles ranging from 3.9mm × 30mm to 3.9mm × 50mm.

◆ **DIN 4 – medium to high security (sensitive documents)**
This level of security can only be achieved with cross-cut shredders that can create very small particles of 1.9mm × 15mm. Sensitive documents that specifically relate to protecting your livelihood or the integrity of a company would require this level of security.

◆ **DIN 5 – high security (top secret documents)**
This level of machine is specifically supplied to government and military locations where it is essential that documents are shredded to preserve national security. As with DIN 4, this can only be achieved with a cross-cut shredder that create extremely small particles of 0.78mm × 11mm.

## IDENTITY FRAUD PROTECTION SERVICES

With the continued rise of identity related crime, banks, credit card companies, insurers and other financial organisations have started to offer a range of identity fraud protection services. These include:

◆ insurance policies
◆ access to your credit report
◆ CIFAS protective registration
◆ Garlik DataPatrol.

### Identity fraud insurance

There has been a mixed reaction to this insurance because

although it is undoubtedly useful if you become a victim of identity fraud, in most cases the services provided can be obtained without the need of a policy. Nevertheless, identity fraud can be a traumatic experience but the peace of mind provided by a policy can be money well spent. Depending on which type of policy you buy and which company you buy from, policies range from around £4 to £7 per month. Although these will help to prevent identity fraud, it is worth remembering that they will not insure you against becoming a victim or compensate you for any money that you may lose to fraudsters. The variety of benefits offered by these policies includes the following.

◆ Financial cover against the cost of reclaiming your identity and restoring your credit rating. This could include legal expenses, loss of wages, telephone calls, rejected loan application fees and postage costs for sending registered mail. The amount of cover offered can vary considerably from £5,000 to £60,000, so it is worth shopping around and reading the policy carefully.

◆ Emergency money if you are temporarily unable to access your bank accounts or use your credit, debit or store cards.

◆ Access to your credit report and notification when any changes are made. Some companies offer unlimited access whereas others will send a monthly or quarterly report.

◆ Credit correction service to help amend your credit file with credit providers and reference agencies.

- Protective registration with CIFAS if any of your personal information becomes lost or stolen, see page 154.

- A personal identify fraud expert to provide professional guidance, advice and support. For complex cases, some companies may arrange to send a dedicated expert to your home.

- A confidential advice line to answer specific identity fraud-related enquiries.

- Document registration and replacement service for valuable documents such as passports and driving licences.

- Registration with Garlik DataPatrol that allows you to monitor and control online places where your personal information is stored by searching the internet for your details. They will also provide regular risk assessment reports and a quarterly credit report, see page 60.

Further information about identity fraud insurance can be obtained from:

CPP Identity Protection
Tel: 0870 121 9187
www.cpp.co.uk/identityprotection/

Identity Care Insurance
Tel: 0870 606 4050
www.identitycare.co.uk

Sentinel Identity Theft Protection
Tel: 0800 414 717
www.sentinelcardprotection.com

Some credit card companies now include free identity fraud assistance as a standard benefit with certain types of card. If you have had your card for a while then it is worth checking with your card provider because this may have been added to your existing benefits. Although identity fraud assistance will not provide financial protection against the cost of reclaiming your identity, it can still be worth having for the specialist expert advice offered through their identity fraud helpline. Alternatively, you may be able to upgrade to financial protection so it's worth contacting your card provider.

### Checking your credit report

One of the best ways to combat identity theft is to regularly check your credit report for any changes that have been made without your knowledge. Your report contains a comprehensive history of any loan, credit card or mortgage application you have made, money you have borrowed and details of your repayment history. This information is used by credit reference agencies to determine your credit rating which is one of the most valuable assets that you have. If your rating is damaged by fraudsters then you will have difficulty securing credit until your rating is fully restored so it is important to protect and safeguard this at all times. This can be achieved by regularly obtaining a copy of your credit report from one of the three credit reference agencies:

Callcredit
One Park Lane, Leeds, LS3 1EP
Automated Helpline: 0870 060 1414
Tel: 0113 244 1555

Fax: 0113 234 0050
www.callcredit.co.uk
www.mycallcredit.com

Equifax
Credit File Advice Centre, PO Box 1140, Bradford, BD1
5US
Tel: 0870 010 0583
www.equifax.co.uk

Experian
Consumer Help Service, PO Box 9000, Nottingham,
NG80 7WP
Tel: 0870 241 6212
www.experian.co.uk

Alternatively, Check My File allows you to choose
between a Single Agency Report from one of the above
agencies, a Triple Agency Report from all three or
Unlimited Access to Triple Agency Reports:

Check My File
Credit Reporting Agency Limited, 13 High Cross, Truro,
TR1 2AJ
Tel: 0800 612 0421
Fax: 0870 094 0069
www.checkmyfile.com

From your report you will be able to immediately see if
your identity has been fraudulently used to set up any
loans or credit accounts. You will also be able to stop any
pending applications, rectify your credit report and

prevent fraudsters from continuing to use your identity. These agencies also offer a range of subscription services that can monitor your report and contact you if there are any changes. Some services permit unlimited access to your report and will also send regular identity theft news together with advice and tips about how to protect yourself. For further information see:

| | |
|---|---|
| MyCallcredit E-Alerts | www.mycallcredit.com |
| Equifax Credit Watch | www.equifax.co.uk |
| Experian CreditExpert | www.experian.co.uk |

### CIFAS Protective Registration

The Credit Industry Fraud Advisory Scheme (CIFAS) is the UK's fraud prevention service. They do not provide a credit reference service but their information is used by fraud prevention agencies and credit reference agencies when any fraudulent activity is suspected. If your personal identification documents have been lost or stolen or if your identity has been used to apply for financial services then you can apply for a Protective Registration notice to be placed on your credit file. This will ensure that further security measures are taken to confirm your identity before approval is granted. For further information, see page 154, Protective Registration From CIFAS or contact:

CIFAS Protective Registration Service
PO Box 1141, Bradford, BD1 5UR
Tel: 0870 010 2091
Email: protective.registrationuk@equifax.com
www.cifas.org.uk

## Garlik DataPatrol

Garlik DataPatrol is a subscription service that monitors the internet for any online places where your personal details could be stored. These range from website entries to public records such as Land Registry, credit files and the Register of Births, Deaths and Marriages. In 1996, no electronic public records were available in the UK but today there are nearly 700 million. Garlik will regularly search these files and records for your details and will send a monthly report listing online places where your personal information has been found. They will also send frequent risk assessment reports together with advice about how to manage and monitor your digital profile and will also notify you of any changes made to your online presence. In addition, quarterly credit reports will also be sent that can be used to identify and rectify any unknown entries that may affect your credit rating. For further information contact Garlik at www.garlik.com

### TOP TEN TIPS TO PROTECT YOUR IDENTITY

✔ Buy a cross-cut shredder and use it to shred old bank statements, card receipts, utility bills, invoices, delivery notes, medical letters, direct mail and any other personal and confidential documents that contain your details.

✔ Never disclose your personal information to anyone that you do not know. This particularly applies if you are unexpectedly contacted by telephone or email.

✔ Always question why you are being asked for personal information and if you have any concerns or doubts, refuse to disclose your details.

✔ Keep your personal and confidential documents secure in a lockable drawer, secure cabinet or safe, or ideally a combination of all three, and only carry these documents with you when it is absolutely necessary.

✔ If you are moving, immediately notify every company and organisation that you deal with to give them your change of address and also arrange with Royal Mail to have your post redirected for at least a year.

✔ When using your credit or debit card, always shield the keypad to conceal your PIN from onlookers and never let your card out of your sight. This particularly applies when paying in a shop, garage or restaurant.

✔ Limit the number of credit or debit cards that you have. Never carry more cards than you need and immediately notify your card provider if they become lost or stolen.

✔ Do not include your date of birth, National Insurance or driving licence number on your CV. There is no need for potential employers to have these and you cannot guarantee how they deal with confidential information.

✔ Register with the Mail Preference Service (MPS), Telephone Preference Service (TPS), Fax Preference Service (FPS) and Email Preference Service (eMPS) to have your personal details removed from sales and marketing lists.

✔ Ensure that any dormant accounts are formally closed because mail order or credit card accounts could easily be reactivated, particularly if they are registered to a previous address.

## VICTIMS' STORIES

### Credit card identity theft

When Darcey became frail, her family arranged for Rebecca

to visit three times a week to clean the house and run the occasional errand. Rebecca got to know Darcey well but, unbeknown to her, Rebecca was gathering as much of Darcey's personal information as she could. In a short period of time, Rebecca had acquired enough information about Darcey to take out several credit cards in her name. By the time the fraud was discovered, Rebecca had amassed debts of over £14,000.

Although Rebecca was arrested and charged with fraud, Darcey's family were left to help her sort out the mess. They arranged for a copy of Darcey's credit report to be sent and used this as a starting point to notify every organisation and company that she had an account with about the fraud. They also arranged for a Protective Registration alert to be placed on her credit reference file to help stop any further applications.

### Postal identity fraud

When Jake moved from one rented property to another he contacted Royal Mail and arranged to have his post redirected to his new address for six months. He also notified every company, organisation and government department that he had an account or dealings with. For nine months everything was fine but then he received a letter from a debt collection agency claiming that he owed over £1,500 to a catalogue company. He thought it must be a mistake and immediately contacted the company. It soon became clear that an account had been set up using just his name and previous address. Even though his date of birth, mother's maiden name and employment details were all incorrect the company still opened a credit account in his name.

After numerous telephone calls and letters, the catalogue company finally believed Jake and agreed not to pursue him for the outstanding debt. Jake was concerned that this could happen again so he applied to CIFAS, the UK's Fraud Prevention Service, for a Protective Registration notice to be placed on his credit reference file. This informs potential lenders that he has been a victim of identity fraud and requests that additional security checks are conducted to prove the credit application is genuine before approval can be granted.

## (3)

# Keeping Your Computer Secure

As the popularity of computing continues to increase, so does the necessity to keep your computer secure. This chapter will provide an overview of how to protect your computer by using passwords to restrict access from unauthorised users and will also explore internet security, firewalls, viruses, spyware and spam. It will also look at creating a secure network, upgrading and updating your computer and the problems associated with peer-to-peer (P2P) file sharing. The chapter will conclude with advice about securely erasing files and folders on your hard drive to prevent them from being fraudulently accessed.

## PROTECTING YOUR COMPUTER

Your computer is an integral part of your identity because it contains enough information to assume your identity and steal from you. This information is highly sought after by criminals and fraudsters so it is important to protect it at all times. Unfortunately, this cannot be achieved with the push of a button or a single computer program. Instead, a variety of procedures and protocols need to be employed to preserve the contents of your computer.

### Controlling access to your computer

At the heart of any computer security system is controlling who can access it and who can access the information that it contains. Besides the obvious threat of anonymous online hackers there is another less considered security risk. Family members, work colleagues and temporary staff can also sabotage, destroy or steal your valuable information unless you restrict their access. Fortunately, this can be inexpensive and relatively easy to implement.

For circumstances when you need to restrict who can physically access your computer then your BIOS (Basic Input Output Setup) settings can be modified to boot-proof your hard drive or password protect your BIOS. You can also enable start-up and screensaver passwords that will restrict access from unauthorised users.

**Boot-proofing your hard drive**
With the assistance of a bootable floppy disc or CD it is possible for an intruder to access and read your hard drive without having to start-up your entire system. In order to avoid this, your BIOS settings can be modified to disable boot devices from your start-up sequence. If this is not possible, then your hard drive can be selected as the primary boot device, which means that your computer will only boot from the hard drive and not from any other source. Alternatively, you could physically remove the floppy and CD/DVD drives and disable or remove any USB or FireWire ports which could also be used to boot your computer from a USB device or FireWire hard disk.

**Password protecting your BIOS**
To prevent your computer being started without your permission it is possible to assign a password to your

BIOS, which means that your system will not start until the correct password is entered. Some newer BIOS systems can also be set to prevent any settings being changed without a password. BIOS passwords are a good security feature but they are not completely secure because some systems accept master passwords that are freely available online. More resourceful intruders can reset passwords by moving a jumper on the motherboard or by disconnecting and reconnecting the power to the BIOS.

## Using biometric log-in devices

As more people start to seriously consider computer security, biometric log-in devices are gradually becoming very popular. They provide an extremely high level of security and, with prices ranging from £30 to £40, they are relatively inexpensive to buy. Some systems combine a biometric fingerprint scanner, with password management and encryption software. This means that with the press of your finger the device can be used to log-on to your system, log-in to websites, encrypt and decrypt files and protect your system from unauthorised users.

## Encrypting your files and folders

Data encryption makes it more difficult for your computer to be accessed from an installation disc, for your passwords to be uncovered or for important information to be stolen. Some operating systems already have data encryption built into them but for others you will need to purchase separate encryption software. Your operating manual should be able to tell you if your system is capable of data encryption and what steps to take. Data encryption is ideal for laptops and other portable devices including hard drives, computer discs and flash memory USB sticks. However, data encryption is very time-consuming, can slow the performance of your computer and can make it more difficult to retrieve lost, damaged or deleted files. Only consider this if you have highly sensitive information to protect. For the majority of computer users, data encryption is unnecessary provided other security measures have been taken.

## USING PASSWORDS

Passwords have become a necessary and important part of everyday life. They are needed to access a variety of systems, accounts and activities including:

* computer systems, programs and files
* credit card accounts and PIN numbers
* websites
* email accounts
* online banking
* telephone banking
* alarm codes
* door entry systems.

Creating a different password for each account is essential to provide a barrier between you and those who want to access your information. However, with so many pass-words to remember there can be a temptation to use the same details more than once. This should be avoided because if your details are discovered then this will compromise every account and system that requires a particular password. This section will look at how passwords are used and will show you how to create, store and protect your passwords.

## Log-in passwords

Most operating systems can be configured to require a log-in password before they can be accessed. This can also be used to lock your computer when you are temporarily away from your desk and do not want to completely shut it down. Log-in passwords are an ideal way to protect your system from intruders and are particularly useful for laptops that can be stolen more easily. If your computer is stolen then at least if you have created a strong log-in password (see below), there is a possibility that the thief will not be able to access the contents immediately. However, a number of password retrieval programs are freely available and can be misused to discover your password.

## Screen saver passwords

As an extra precautionary measure, enable a password-protected screen saver to automatically activate and log-off the system if your computer is idle for a set period of time. This means that a casual passer-by will be unable to use your computer during your absence. Some people find that five minutes is an adequate delay while others consider 15 minutes to be more reasonable but this will depend on your work pattern.

## Creating strong passwords

Regardless of the information that they protect, passwords should always be as strong as possible and, fortunately, creating a strong password is a relatively simple process. The strength of your password will depend on a number of contributory factors such as the length and random combination of characters used. Your password should ideally be no less than eight characters long but passwords of 14 or more characters are better because they provide a greater level of protection. The strongest passwords are those that use the entire keyboard and appear to look like a random string of upper and lower case letters, numbers, keyboard symbols and punctuation marks.

In addition, some password systems also permit the use of the space bar which means that lengthy phrases, known as passphrases, can be used. These are often easier to remember than specific passwords and can also be more difficult to crack. When deciding on a passphrase, always choose a sentence that you can easily remember but will be difficult for others to guess, for example, a line from your favourite book, poem or song. To further strengthen your password, spell words incorrectly, mix upper and lower case letters and include numbers.

Alternatively, if your password system does not support passphrases then simply create an acronym password (mnemonic) whereby the first letter of each word is used to create an unintelligible word that will be difficult to decipher. Once again, mix upper and lowercase letters and include numbers. For example, 'Three blind mice, see how they run' could become '3BmsHtR'. As a final check, consider checking the strength of your password with an online password checker. Microsoft have a very good one that does not retain or distribute any checked passwords. Microsoft Password Checker available at

www.microsoft.com/protect/yourself/password/checker.
mspx

## Passwords to avoid

When creating a password there are some sequences and
combinations that should always be avoided because they
will only create weak passwords that can be easily
cracked. These include the following.

*Repeated, sequential or adjacent keyboard characters*
Combinations such as 'aaaaaa', '123456' or 'qwerty' are
very weak.

*Dictionary words or regular names*
Even if these are spelled incorrectly or backwards they can
easily be uncovered with one of the many cracking tools
used by hackers.

*Personal information*
Your name, log-in name, date of birth, telephone numbers,
previous street names, favourite teams, mother's maiden
name, pet's name, names of family members or any of their
personal details can be easily guessed.

*Single words with common character replacements*
Predictable replacements such as an 'a' for an '@' and an
'o' with a '0' as in 'p@ssw0rd', or an 'e' for a '3' and an 'i'
for a '1' as in 'wh1sk3y' are already known to hackers.

*The same password more than once*
This is never a good idea because if a hacker discovers
your password then they will be able to access any other
system with the same password.

*Blank passwords*

Some operating systems such as Windows XP allows you to assign blank passwords to your accounts. This can be useful if you only have one computer and you trust everyone who has access to it or you have several computers but you do not need to exchange information between them. Surprisingly, blank passwords are more secure than weak ones because your user accounts cannot be externally accessed without first creating a password but they are not generally recommended as a security measure. This particularly applies to laptops which should always have strong passwords assigned to them.

## Protecting your passwords

Passwords are as important as any other personal information you have and protecting them should always be of paramount importance. Listed below are a number of common sense approaches you can employ to ensure passwords remain protected at all times.

*Always keep passwords to yourself*

Never reveal your passwords to anyone because this will jeopardise the information that they have been created to protect. This particularly applies to children who may inadvertently pass them on to their friends or unscrupulous individuals. The only exception to this would be the necessity to access non-sensitive shared files in a corporate environment or shared accounts with a spouse or partner who you trust.

*Never respond to unsolicited password requests*

Any correspondence that you receive to verify your password will invariably be a scam, so never reply under any circumstances. Genuine companies will never request information in this way. If you have any doubts then always raise your concerns with the company directly. This should always be on a publicly advertised number and not through any details contained within the correspondence, because these will undoubtedly be false.

### Regularly change your passwords

Never become complacent about your passwords and assume that they will always be secure. The stronger your passwords are then the greater the interval between changing them. In general terms, a strong password of eight characters or less should be updated on a weekly basis, whereas a password of 14 characters or more should be updated annually.

### Disable auto complete

Your web browser has a handy function called auto complete that can be used to complete web page addresses, forms and usernames and passwords on forms. Although this can be useful for commonly used fields such as your name, address, telephone number and email address, it can also present a security risk. This particularly applies if your computer is used or accessed by other users because they will be able to use your details automatically without having to know your exact details. From a security point of view it is advisable to disable this feature, for further information, see page 74, Internet Security.

### Never use a public or networked computer to access password-protected data

Public or networked computers should always be avoided to access any sensitive data that requires your password.

This is because fraudsters can easily install key logging programs that can remotely recall your log-in details and passwords. Password-sensitive information should only be accessed through your own protected personal computer that is as secure as possible. Your passwords are as valuable as the data that they protect and fraudsters will pay to access this information.

## Storing your passwords

With the necessity to have so many different passwords, remembering all of them can prove difficult. Therefore, it is probably necessary to store them safely and securely for retrieval at a later date. There are different ways to do this (as listed below), but deciding which is best for you will be depend on how comfortable you are with how they are stored.

*Install a password management program on your computer*

Programs such as RoboForm (www.roboform.com), Comodo i-Vault (www.comodo.com) and Access Manager (www.accessmanager.co.uk) are available to download for free, whereas programs such as Norton Password Manager (www.symantec.com), My Security Vault Pro (www.whitecanyon.com) and SplashID Password Safe (www.splashdata.com) can be purchased from most computer retailers. These programs create a digital vault on your computer to store passwords that can only be opened with a master password.

*Install a password management program on your USB flash drive*

This works in the same way as the above systems but your passwords are stored on a portable device that can be carried with you at all times.

*Register your passwords with a web-based provider*
Providers such as Password Manager Pro (http://manage engine.adventnet.com) and Passlet (www.passlet.com) offer web-based password registration services. These work in a similar way to storing your passwords on your computer but these companies will have more secure security systems.

*Write them down on a piece of paper*
This controversial method is the simplest and easiest way to store your passwords and, contrary to public opinion, providing these are kept in a safe place, is no less secure than electronically storing them on your computer or with a web-based provider. This system cannot be compromised over the internet so the potential for theft is limited to the number of people who have access to where they are kept.

## Stolen passwords
Regardless of which method you use, no single password storage system is completely secure but by creating strong passwords that are changed regularly then the possibility of your password being stolen is greatly reduced. However, if any of your passwords are stolen then you need to be aware of this as soon as it happens. This can only be achieved by regularly checking the information that they protect and immediately contacting the relevant organisation if there is any suspicious activity on any of your accounts.

## INTERNET SECURITY
Despite the many benefits that the internet has to offer there are also many threats that you need to be aware of. Criminals and fraudsters are constantly trying to find

ways to steal your money, your identity or the contents of your computer. Fortunately, it is relatively easy to protect yourself and your computer when you are online. In order to access the internet, you will need a browser which comes pre-installed with every commercially bought computer system.

Popular browsers include Microsoft Internet Explorer, Mozilla Firefox and Opera. Whichever you use, it is always important to upgrade to the latest version because this will provide the best level of protection. You can find out which version you are running by clicking the Help button on your browser's toolbar and selecting About. Some browsers can be configured to automatically upgrade to the latest version whereas others need to be manually updated. Upgrades should always be downloaded directly from the browser's main website and not from a third-party website because you can never be too sure exactly what you are downloading. Internet browsers have a number of built-in security features but you may need to alter their default settings to maximise your protection.

### Anti-phishing protection

Phishing occurs when you are asked to confirm your username, log-in, bank or credit card details at what appears to be a genuine financial website. However, these websites have been created by fraudsters to acquire your personal details and steal your money. Anti-phishing filters cross-reference the website you are visiting against a list of suspected sites and trigger an alert if the site is on the list. Some browsers have an anti-phishing risk-rating bar that gradually changes from green to red depending on the phishing risk associated with the website. Websites that generate a predominately red bar should always be avoided.

## Dealing with cookies

Cookies are small files that some websites create on your computer with details about how you use their site. Some browsers allow you to control how each cookie is dealt with. Others only allow you to reject or accept all cookies or to accept cookies from websites that you have previously visited. The various privacy settings include:

◆ **Block all cookies**
  This setting will block all cookies from the website you are visiting and will also prevent existing cookies on your computer from being read by the original website that created them.

◆ **High**
  All cookies that do not have a compact privacy policy and all cookies that use personally identifiable information without your explicit consent will be blocked.

◆ **Medium**
  This setting will block third-party cookies that do not have a compact privacy policy and third-party cookies that use personally identifiable information without your explicit consent. In addition, first-party cookies that use personally identifiable information without your implicit consent will be restricted.

◆ **Low**

Third-party cookies that do not have a compact privacy policy and third-party cookies that use personally identifiable information without your implicit consent will be restricted.

◆ **Accept all cookies**

This setting will permit all cookies to be saved on your computer and permit existing cookies to be read by the website that created them.

### Avoid auto complete

Most browsers give you the option to automatically complete entries on websites from previously entered information. This includes search boxes, the address bar, usernames, passwords and all kinds of other personal information. Although this saves time and removes the necessity to constantly re-type the same information, it can present a huge security risk. This is because if your computer is used by somebody else then they can see what you have searched for and which websites you have visited. They could also access your accounts without needing to know your precise log-in details.

Fortunately, this information can be cleared from your internet history by selecting the Clear function from the internet Options or Properties menu of your browser. You can also choose to disable auto complete partially or completely. This can be useful if you want to save your search history but not your usernames and passwords. The configuration options you are usually given include the following:

- **Web addresses**

  When this option is enabled you will be able to retrieve the full website address by entering just the first few letters into your address bar.

- **Forms**

  This option will retrieve any previously entered information that has been entered into a form such as your name, address and telephone number.

- **Usernames and passwords**

  If this option is enabled, all of your usernames and passwords will be stored on your computer. This option is not recommended because, even if you are the only person who can access your computer, it could be stolen and thieves will be able to access your private websites.

### Disabling JavaScript

JavaScript is a type of computer programming language that web developers use to make their websites more interactive. Most of these programs are perfectly harmless but some malicious websites can use JavaScript to gain access to your computer. This is why it is important to only visit trusted sites and to use your browser to identify potentially fraudulent sites. Some browsers allow you to disable JavaScript and other plug-ins, such as ActiveX, that some websites use to enhance their graphics. Alternatively, you could use a browser such as Firefox or Opera that does not support ActiveX.

### Website restrictions

Most browsers can be configured to control how a

computer responds to certain websites. For example, access can be restricted to websites with known security issues and, conversely, access can be authorised to genuine websites that you trust not to damage your computer. This security feature gives you more control over how you use the internet and the websites that you visit.

### Anti-spyware protection

When enabled, spyware filters can be configured to warn you when a website attempts to download, install or run software. For more information about what spyware is and how to deal with it, see page 87, Spyware.

### Pop-up windows

These are the small annoying boxes that sometimes appear when you log-on to certain websites. Although they are often advertisements or links to other websites they can also be used to steal information, take control of your home page and install spyware or adware. Not all pop-ups are harmful, some contain important information that you may need to respond to. For example, before your computer will download a file or install new software a pop-up window will often appear prompting you for permission to continue. Therefore, it is important to manage how your computer deals with these by configuring your pop-up preferences. The range of options you will be given usually include allowing all pop-ups, blocking all pop-ups or only allowing pop-ups on trusted sites.

## FIREWALLS

The internet is essentially a network of connected computers which means that, when connected, any computer can potentially find and connect to any other computer. This can prove disastrous, particularly if a hacker gains access to your computer and all the files that it contains. With access to your computer a hacker can see which files you open, which passwords you use, which bank accounts you have and which credit cards you use. With this information, a hacker can transfer money from your accounts, steal your identity or use your computer to send spam and other malicious emails that appear to come from you.

However, by installing a firewall you can partially protect your computer from hackers and some viruses. Firewalls work as a barrier between your computer and the millions of computers that collectively comprise the internet. There is a commonly-held belief that if you have a firewall then you are fully protected from online threats but this is simply not true. Firewalls will not protect you from spam, spyware and the majority of viruses. They also offer limited or no protection if:

◆ your firewall has been disabled or switched off

◆ permission has been granted for other computers to access your computer

◆ a virus has created a back door into your computer that bypasses the firewall

◆ a hacker has acquired the password to your firewall.

Firewalls are an important part of computer security but they do not offer complete security as a standalone product. They are only effective if they are used in conjunction with other protective programs such as anti-virus software. For further information, see page 84, Types of anti-virus software.

## Types of firewall

When considering which type of firewall is best suited to your needs, it is important to recognise the strengths and weaknesses of the options open to you. There are three main types of firewall to choose from:

- a desktop firewall
- a commercial firewall
- a hardware firewall.

### *Desktop firewalls*

These are also known as software firewalls and are installed on each computer that is able to connect to the internet. They are designed to monitor and, if necessary, block or restrict the flow of internet traffic between your computer and the internet. Desktop firewalls need to be configured to work with your computer by learning which programs are used to connect to the internet. When the firewall is switched on, a pop-up warning will appear when a new program attempts to connect to the internet for the first time. How you respond to these messages will determine how your firewall is configured. Therefore, it is important to only permit legitimate programs to connect. If you are unsure about the program then always decline permission until you can verify the origin.

Most computers come with a pre-installed firewall as part of the initial software package that will provide a certain amount of protection. However, for a more comprehensive firewall package you will need to upgrade to a commercial desktop firewall or a hardware firewall.

### Commercial firewalls

Commercial firewalls work in a similar way to desktop firewalls in that they are individually installed on each computer that can access the internet. They monitor applications that connect to the internet in order to prevent Trojans, keyloggers, back doors and other malware from entering your computer. The main benefit of commercial firewalls is that they can be regularly updated to provide greater protection against new online threats. They can also be individually configured which will allow greater control and flexibility over how the firewall works. Commercial firewalls are available as either a standalone product or, more commonly, as part of a larger security suite. Standalone programs that can be downloaded for free include:

Comodo Firewall Pro     www.personalfirewall.comodo.com
PC Tools Firewall Plus            www.pctools.com
ZoneAlarm                     www.zonealarm.com

Alternatively, the following security suites include a firewall as an integral part of the program:

Kaspersky Internet Security        www.kaspersky.com
McAfee Internet Security Suite      www.mcafee.co.uk
Norton Internet Security          www.symantec.com

### Hardware firewalls

Whereas desktop and commercial firewalls need to be installed on each computer with access to the internet, a hardware firewall allows a number of computers to be protected through a shared internet connection. This is generally how most business networks operate but even a small home network can be set up in this way. Most internet routers have a hardware firewall device built into them but they can sometimes prove more difficult to set up than desktop or commercial firewalls. However, most suppliers provide telephone support and, in some cases, they can arrange for an engineer to call and install the router for you. This will usually incur an additional charge but it could be worth the expense, particularly if you are unfamiliar with how to configure a firewall.

## VIRUSES

Computer viruses work in many different ways, some are designed to cause maximum damage by wiping your hard drive or installing offensive material and some will even lock you out of your computer. Anti-virus software is one of the most important protective programs that can be installed on your computer. It works by constantly scanning for viruses that can infiltrate and infect your computer. These include incoming emails with infected attachments, viruses released when documents are opened and viruses that attack over the internet.

However, the most dangerous type of virus is those that bury themselves deep within your computer and remain undetected. These can create a back door for hackers to access your system, automatically copy and send sensitive data or record your internet activity including your computer keystrokes. With this information hackers can discover your passwords, steal your identity and make purchases in your name. Anti-virus programs are just one type of security measure but as a single product they will not completely protect you from hackers, most spyware, spam and any virus for which it does not have a signature. Therefore, they are best used in conjunction with other protective programs such as firewalls, anti-spyware and anti-spam filtering.

## Types of anti-virus software

As with firewalls, there are a number of options open to you when choosing which type of anti-virus software is best suited to your needs. For example, they are available as either standalone products or as part of a larger security suite that can either be downloaded for free or purchased. The main difference is that whereas standalone programs will only scan for viruses, security suites also include additional protective programs such as firewalls, anti-spyware and anti-spam filtering.

The main benefits of a security suite are that they are relatively easy to use, all of the programs are designed to work with each other and they can all be accessed through a central interface. However, although this is a cost-efficient way of buying a comprehensive range of protective programs, it is worth considering just how effective these additional programs are. Security suites usually have a very good anti-virus program but sometimes the other programs are not as good as those individually available from other suppliers. A security suite is ideal for those new to computer security but as you become more familiar with the programs on offer you may choose to buy other programs from individual suppliers.

*How they work*

Whenever new viruses are released, they are analysed by security firms who develop a counter-program to render them ineffective before assigning a unique anti-virus signature to them. These signatures are used by anti-virus programs to identify and block new viruses before they can penetrate your computer. In order to be effective, it is important that your anti-virus software is kept up to date, otherwise it will not be able to detect new threats as they become available. Most programs can be set to automatically check for updates whilst others provide pop-up reminders.

## Getting anti-virus software

When you have decided which type of anti-virus software is best for you, the next step is to decide whether to buy or download the programs you need for free. If you choose to buy, most manufacturers will include an initial one-year subscription within the purchase price. This means that you will be able to regularly download the latest virus signatures and security updates to ensure that your computer is fully protected. At the end of the year you can either renew your subscription or buy a different product.

Alternatively, a variety of programs are available to download for free. However, these are either trial versions of full programs or they are similar to commercial products but they have limited functionality. Trial versions will usually have some of their features disabled and will only work for a short period of time before you will need to purchase a licence to continue using them. Similarly, free programs are often basic versions of their commercial counterparts and their technical support is either very limited or non-existent. The best solution is to buy a commercial product with full technical support because these manufacturers have the financial resources to research and further develop their products.

### General anti-virus advice

After you have installed an anti-virus program it doesn't mean you can become complacent and let your software do all the work. There are many preventive actions that still need to be taken to help your software help you, these include the following.

◆ **Never open email attachments from an unknown source**
Your anti-virus program should have identified and quarantined the attachment as a potential threat but it always pays to exercise extreme caution when dealing with email attachments.

◆ **Regularly run a full system virus scan**
Some websites offer free online anti-virus scans. These are useful to identify potential threats but they are not as comprehensive as an installed anti-virus program and should not be relied upon to protect your computer. In fact, some programs will only identify viruses without removing potential threats until you have purchased the full version.

◆ **Enable macro protection**
Most office applications offer this option which should always be switched on because viruses can often be concealed in macros that are activated with email attachments.

◆ **Use the pre-installed anti-virus trial program**
Most computers come with an anti-virus program pre-installed. This will usually be a fully functional trial version but at the end of the trial period you will need to pay a subscription in order to stay protected or buy another anti-virus program.

◆ **Never install more that one anti-virus program at a time**
Anti-virus programs can conflict with one another and not work properly, which will leave your computer vulnerable to attack.

## SPYWARE

Spyware programs are very similar to viruses from the perspective that they are installed without your knowledge or your permission. They are often embedded within other programs and applications such as internet downloads, peer-to-peer file sharing and email attachments, which make them extremely difficult but not impossible to remove. Some spyware can be identified, quarantined and destroyed with a good anti-virus package but the majority will remain undetected unless you use a dedicated anti-spyware program.

### Adware spyware

Not all spyware programs are the same, they come in a variety of different formats with a variety of different objectives. At the lower end of the spyware scale are adware programs, which create pop-up adverts to direct you to specific websites. These are often gambling or pornographic websites which can be extremely offensive particularly if accidentally viewed by young children. Some adverts are created within the code of the spyware but others will download specific advertisements from the internet. Other uses for adware include installing new desktop icons, creating new browser menus and toolbar buttons, changing your homepage and changing your internet search engine.

This means that when you click on either a new icon or a new toolbar button or follow a link from your new search engine it is highly likely that your browsing habits are being externally monitored. This data will then be used to generate further advertisements specifically targeted towards your personal interests. Adware can also be used to restrict access to specific websites, persuade you to disable your existing anti-virus or anti-spyware programs and deny access to subsequent updates.

### Surveillance spyware

At the other end of the scale is surveillance spyware which, as the name implies, is designed to remain undetected on your computer. These stealth programs are the most dangerous and intrusive types of spyware because they can be used to secretly acquire your personal, security and identity information. They work by covertly scanning your computer for your personal information such as passwords and credit card details and then upload this data to criminals. This is achieved by recording your keystrokes and capturing screen shots of websites you have visited that clearly contain your personal data.

### Avoiding spyware

An unprotected computer can be infected with a number of different spyware programs all running at the same time. This can result in your computer becoming slow and unreliable by crashing on a regular basis. To reduce the possibility of inadvertently installing spyware there are a number of preventative steps you can take, as follows.

- **Only buy and install genuine software from reputable suppliers**
  Never install counterfeit software and always avoid downloading programs over peer-to-peer file sharing networks.

- **Only download free software from websites that operate a strict no-spyware policy**
  In reality these websites will probably have a disclaimer to indemnify themselves against spyware accidentally being downloaded but at least they are making a concerted effort to try to eradicate spyware from their programs.

- **Always monitor the installation process when downloading free software**
  This will help to ensure that you not installing additional spyware programs. The permission to install these is often contained within the licence agreement that you must agree to before the installation process can begin. So always read the licence carefully and never simply click on the *I Agree* button.

- **Never click on an advertisement offering a free spyware scan**
  These advertisements often contain spyware and the scan will always 'find' spyware on your computer that can only be deleted if you buy their spyware removal program.

## Anti-spyware programs

Anti-spyware programs work in a similar way to anti-virus programs by scanning for known spyware signatures and preventing new spyware infections. The majority of commercial Internet Security Suites including Kaspersky, McAfee and Norton have anti-spyware programs contained within them.

| | |
|---|---|
| Kaspersky Internet Security | www.kaspersky.com |
| McAfee Internet Security Suite | www.mcafee.co.uk |
| Norton Internet Security | www.symantec.com |

In addition to these, a number of standalone programs are also available that can be bought or downloaded for free, these include:

| | |
|---|---|
| Ad-Aware | www.lavasoftusa.com |
| Spyware Doctor | www.pctools.com |
| Spyware Terminator | www.spywareterminator.com |

Alternatively, the following programs can also be purchased:

| | |
|---|---|
| NoAdware | www.noadware.net |
| Webroot Spy Sweeper | www.digitaldriver.com |
| XoftSpySE | www.paretologic.com |

## SPAM

Spam is the name given to unsolicited emails that regularly fill up your inbox. It is estimated that up to 90% of the billions of emails sent each day are sent by spammers and are usually advertisements for cheap medicines, enlargement surgery, pornographic websites, money-making schemes, gambling websites or counterfeit software.

Fortunately, most people are aware of the unbelievable claims made by some spam mail and know not to respond. However, because millions of emails can be sent at the touch of a button for next to no cost, spammers only need a very small percentage of people to reply to make them profitable. The golden rules when dealing with spam are to never respond, never buy from spam advertisements and never be tempted to make charitable donations because your money will go directly to the spammer. If you do want to donate to charity then always contact the charity through an advertised number or by typing their web address directly into your internet browser.

### Reducing spam

It is unlikely that spam will ever be totally eliminated but with careful forethought and planning you can actively reduce the amount of spam you receive. The first step is to create a main email address that is difficult for spammers or automated software programs to guess. This should be a long combination of letters, numbers and punctuation marks that should only be given to people you know. For all other email correspondence, consider setting up a disposable email address that can be easily discarded when the spam becomes too great.

Your email address is an important part of your identity and should be treated just like any other piece of personal information. You would probably think twice about giving your home address to complete strangers so remember to exercise the same caution with your email address. Always think carefully before passing it on to anyone and protect it wherever possible. When choosing an email provider, look for one that offers email filtering as standard. Email filtering is used to automatically identify and sort potential spam by scanning your inbox for key words such as advertisement, extra income, order now or cards accepted.

If your email provider does not offer email filtering then either switch to a company that does or consider using a separate filter program. Programs such as McAfee Spam Killer (www.spamkiller.com) and Ella for Spam Control (www.openfieldsoftware.com) work very well. As an extra precautionary measure, regularly check the status of your email filters because some computer viruses have been known to disable them. This can be done by clicking the Options button and looking for Spam Protection or Junk E-Mail Protection.

In addition to sending advertisements, spam can also be used to perpetuate internet fraud through phishing, see page 114, Types of Internet Fraud. Phishing involves setting up a website that appears to look like a genuine online business such as a bank or a shop. Visitors are encouraged to confirm their personal details after receiving an email warning them to act immediately but the information is captured by fraudsters.

Some spammers have been known to offer spam opt-out services that work in a similar way to the Mail Preference Service (MPS) or Telephone Preference Service (TPS). This is freely available from the Email Preference Service (eMPS) and anyone trying to sell you this service is either trying to get your money, your personal details or both. For more information contact Email Preference Service (eMPS) at www.dmachoice.org/EMPS/

## Dealing with spam

If you receive a just few unwanted emails a day and you do not have an email filter then you may choose to manually sort your inbox. This is usually just a case of scanning through the sender's address and seeing if there is a name you do not recognise. This does not necessarily mean that it is spam, just that you need to exercise caution when dealing with it. When sorting your inbox, remember never to open an unsolicited email or click on a link because you can never be sure where it may take you. This is particularly important when dealing with attachments because they might contain a virus or spyware.

The performance of your email filter can be greatly improved if you train it to identify spam emails that were missed. To do this, never click on Remove or Delete because your filter will just treat the email the same way next time. Instead, select the email and click on the Spam button, the filter will then add the sender's details to its Blocked list. Conversely, you can also train your filter to identify genuine emails that were originally identified as spam by simply selecting the email and clicking on the Not Spam button, the filter will then add the sender's details to its Safe Senders list. On occasion, some email filters can accidentally filter genuine emails so it is important to regularly check your junk folders.

### How spammers get your email address

Spam emails are sent randomly to millions of email addresses on a daily basis and spammers use a variety of different methods to get them. These include:

◆ **Using search tools to find addresses embedded within published web pages**
These are similar to those used by search engines and if your email address is listed on a public website you will probably be inundated with spam because it will be found easily and exploited by spammers.

◆ **Running automated software programs**
These systematically work through all variations of letters, numbers and punctuation marks to try to guess your email address. These programs begin with names and common words so try to avoid using them. Instead chose an obscure combination of letters, numbers and punctuation marks and remember that the longer the address the more difficult it is for spammers to guess.

◆ **Buying email address lists from other spammers or crooked website owners**
This is why it is a good idea to use a disposable address when registering for services or buying from websites.

◆ **Setting up a fake spam email blocking service**
This a free service so the spammer is either trying to get money or your personal details.

## COMPUTER NETWORKING

There was a time when computer networks were only used by businesses or technically minded people. The average family did not want, did not need or could not afford more than one computer, so home networks were considered a luxury. In recent years the cost of computing has been dramatically reduced, which has resulted in more computers being sold than ever before. This has meant that computers have become a large part of everyday life and are now being used for everything from shopping and banking to music, games, videos, instant messaging and school work. With so many different functions, people are finding that one computer can no longer accommodate their needs so most homes have two or more computers. Therefore, creating a secure home network has become a necessity rather than a luxury.

### Creating a secure network

A network enables two or more computers to share files, documents, printers, scanners, CD/DVD burners, music, games, videos and the internet. The two most popular ways to do this are through a WiFi (wireless) or an Ethernet (wired) connection and there are many advantages and disadvantages to each. Although WiFi networks are flexible and relatively inexpensive to set up they are slower and less secure. Conversely, Ethernet networks are faster and more secure but each computer needs to be connected with individual leads which can be both restrictive and unsightly.

Both types of network require a router to connect all the computers. A router is used to direct, exchange and share information and, if it is connected to a modem, then the network can also be used to share an internet connection.

Any network that connects to the internet will require a firewall (see page 79, Firewalls) to protect computers from hackers, viruses, spyware and other online threats. Some routers include a hardware firewall as part of the installation package whereas others require a separate software firewall. Whichever method you use, it is important that your firewall is always switched on and is always kept up to date.

## Configuring a secure network

In its simplest form, configuring a secure network involves encrypting information and controlling who can access it. This can be achieved by physically connecting leads between each computer or by installing a wireless network. To avoid trailing unsightly leads most people choose to install a WiFi network. Although these are convenient, they are also a potential security risk because they can be easily accessed unless they are protected.

## Ethernet (wired) networks

These types of network, can be inexpensive to install if you have only two computers and they are relatively close together because you will only need a Network Interface Card (NIC) in each computer and a cable to connect them. For larger networks you will also need an Ethernet router and a separate cable to connect each device. Ethernet cabling is quite expensive so if your computers are in different parts of the house then a large wired network can be costly to install. To avoid unsightly leads, Ethernet cables can be installed in the walls but this is more commonly found in newly-built houses. However, with the ability to move data faster and more securely than a wireless network, this can be a worthwhile expense particularly if you regularly transfer a lot of files.

### WiFi (wireless) networks

This is the simplest and least expensive way to connect your computers and devices. They are flexible and free from wires but they are also slower and less secure than wired networks so you will need to ensure they are fully protected. WiFi networks use radio waves instead of wires to transmit and receive data which is very similar to the technology found in televisions, cordless phones, radios, mobile phones and walkie-talkies. These networks use 802.11 networking standards and transmit data at frequencies of 2.4 GHz or 5GHz:

| Network standard | Frequency (GHz) | Speed (megabits per second) |
|:---:|:---:|:---:|
| 802.11a | 5 | 54 |
| 802.11b | 2.4 | 11 |
| 802.11g | 2.4 | 54 |

To build a WiFi network you will need a wireless router and a wireless adapter for each computer and device connected to your network. Many new computers have wireless adapters built into them but, for others, they can be connected to a USB port, PC card slot or PCI slot. The average wireless router has an approximate range of 100 feet (30.5 metres) but doors and walls can reduce the strength of the signal. Depending on the shape and size of your house you may also need to buy a signal repeater or range extender to increase the strength and range of your network.

## Protecting your wireless network

An unprotected network is a huge security risk because any computer within range that has a wireless adapter can potentially connect to it. This means that fraudsters and criminals can access your computer from a distance without your knowledge or permission. They can also use your internet connection to download or send material which could get you into trouble because it can be traced back to your computer. Therefore, it is important to configure your network to reduce the possibility of access by unauthorised users. This can be achieved by:

* encrypting your network and controlling who has access
* using access points
* adjusting your privacy settings
* using a firewall.

## Encrypting your network and controlling access

Data encryption is an essential part of network security but when wireless network equipment is first installed the encryption settings will not be activated. This is to ensure that your network is easy to set up. Most equipment will give you the option to use an installation wizard which is highly recommended because it will lead you through the entire process and explain your various options along the way. You can also refer to the set up instructions that came with your equipment which will either be a printed booklet or included on your installation CD.

Your wireless network equipment will have a variety of security options but the first step is to choose which type of encryption is best suited to your needs. There are currently three types of encryption methods to choose between but which ones are available will depend on your equipment and your operating system.

*Wired Equivalent Privacy (WEP)*

This is usually found on older network cards and access points and was originally developed to provide a similar level of protection to a wired network. WEP networks use either 64-bit or 128-bit encryption but they are generally considered the weakest type of security because they use a numerical password which is relatively easy to crack. Hackers can capture and sample network traffic which they can use to acquire your password and access your system.

*WiFi Protected Access (WPA, WPA-PSK and WPA2)*

WPA is the newest and strongest type of encryption that uses a Temporal Key Integrity Protocol (TKIP) to regularly update and change your encryption key. This means that even if hackers capture and sample your network traffic, the information is useless because your encryption key is constantly changing. WPA-PSK is the next best type of encryption, which is supported by most routers. Pre-Shared Key (PSK) authentication works by sharing the same password to securely exchange information between systems. WPA2 offers the highest level of security and introduces the new Advanced Encryption Standard (AES) which is considered fully secure but is only found on the latest hardware.

*Media Access Control (MAC) address filtering*

Unlike WEP or WPA, this type of authentication does not rely on a password to verify users. Instead, it uses the unique 12-digit MAC address that can be found on all network equipment. This means that your network can be accessed only by machines with a specific MAC address that you have added and approved.

### Passphrase technology

As an additional level of security most routers support passphrase technology to generate an encryption key. This allows you to create a random string of characters from a sequence of words or text that are used to control access to your network, see page 68, Creating strong passwords.

### Using an Access Point network

When installing your network you will be asked to choose a network type, which will either be a Computer-to-Computer (Ad Hoc) or an Access Point (Infrastructure). Computer-to-Computer networks, which are also known as peer-to-peer, are less secure than Access Point networks because they exchange data and manage themselves without using a central access point. This means that your computer becomes both a server and a client whereby other computers can access your computer and you can access other computers. Computer-to-Computer networks are typically used to share music, video, software and files over the internet.

Access Point networks are more secure than Computer-to-Computer networks because they create an infrastructure of authorised computers that manage and share information through routers and firewalls. This gives you more control over your network by restricting access to only recognised and trusted computers. This is obviously good from a security perspective.

### Adjusting your privacy settings

During the installation process you will also be given the option to change the name of your Service Set Identifier (SSID). This is simply the name assigned to your network and the default setting will usually be the manufacturer's name. The SSID should be changed to something obscure and the Broadcast SSID option should be switched off. This will make it more difficult for hackers to find and attempt to access your network.

### Using a firewall

In addition to the firewall installed on your router, it is advisable to protect each networked computer with a desktop firewall. This will act as a secondary line of defence and will further strengthen the security of your network. For further information, see page 79, Firewalls.

### One last word

An important point to remember is that your network protection is only as strong as the password that has been used to create it. So always use a strong password and always ensure that your security settings are set to the highest level. For further information, see page 67, Using Passwords.

## UPGRADING AND UPDATING

The electronics industry is constantly evolving to meet changing market trends and the computer hardware sector is no exception. As soon as a product becomes available it is not long before it is superseded by something new and improved. Computer software takes a very long time to develop and during this period the industry and the market will change. Some companies address this by issuing interim updates to their existing software, whereas others will release a completely new and updated version.

Regularly upgrading and updating your software is advantageous because you will be able benefit from the improvements made to the product. These may include fixing bugs, adding extra features, improving performance and protection against some viruses. When you first install new software, it is important to register your product with the company and, in fact, some programs will not work until they are registered. As a newly-registered user you may be entitled to download a future release for free or you may be offered special rates to buy later upgrades.

### Installing patches and updates

Commercial software companies spend huge sums of money developing their products to ensure they work perfectly. Software is only released when manufacturers and developers are confident that their products are free from bugs but hackers endeavour to uncover these. Bugs can be exploited by hackers to create a back door into your computer. This is achieved by creating and releasing viruses that specifically attack systems that use a particular type of software.

When a bug is detected, software companies work hard to solve the problem by developing and issuing update patches. Providing you are using genuine software then these can be downloaded and installed directly from the company's website. Although update patches are designed to improve the performance of the software and address any security issues they should not be treated as a security solution in their own right. Update patches are only effective if they are used in conjunction with firewall, anti-virus and anti-spyware programs. As new versions of software programs become available then these patches become incorporated into the new release.

### Updating your operating system

At the heart of every computer is the operating system which is the part that makes everything else work. The most popular systems are Windows, Mac and Linux and the latest version of each will obviously be the most up to date and the most secure. Operating systems are not released as often as other types of software but manufacturers will frequently release patches and updates. Keeping up to date with these can be difficult but some systems will allow you to automatically download and install updates as soon as they become available. The best way to do this is to visit the download section of the manufacturer's website and follow the update instructions. Before downloading any updates always check that your anti-virus program is up to date and fully enabled.

## PEER-TO-PEER (P2P) FILE SHARING

Peer-to-peer (P2P) file sharing has been a popular online activity since 1999 when Napster was first released. Napster allowed users to freely share MP3 music files over the internet but due to copyright laws, the website was initially ordered to close. It has since been re-launched offering a legitimate pay-for-download service. There are now a number of other P2P programs that can be used to share videos, images, documents and software files, these include:

| | |
|---|---|
| Bearshare | www.bearshare.com |
| BitTorrent | www.bittorrent.com |
| Gnutella | www.gnutella.com |
| iMesh | www.imesh.com |
| Kazaa | www.kaza.com |
| Limewire | www.limewire.com |
| Morpheus | http://morpheus.com |
| Napster | www.napster.co.uk |
| Shareaza | www.shareaza.com |

File-sharing programs need be treated with caution because they present a variety of security and legal issues that you need to be aware of.

## Security issues

From a security perspective these programs are vulnerable to hackers, viruses, adware and spyware. This is because in order to share files, your firewall needs to be configured to permit your P2P program to access the internet. Hackers can exploit these programs to directly access your computer or they can use a virus to create a back door into your system. Adware and spyware programs can often be installed with the main file-sharing program but, fortunately, most P2P programs now claim to be free from adware and spyware and some even allow you to safely scan your downloaded files for viruses.

## Legal issues

The legal concerns of file-sharing programs relate to the exchange of copyrighted material without the owner's permission. Downloading software, music and videos for free can seem very tempting but this activity is illegal because royalties are not paid to the copyright owners. Record companies and artists have taken legal action against those who regularly download their material and many users have been prosecuted and substantially fined. In turn, this has led to the development of programs to conceal your IP address and prevent your personal details being collected without your permission, these include:

| | |
|---|---|
| No-IP Plus | www.no-ip.com |
| PeerGuardian | http://phoenixlabs.org/pg2/ |
| Private Proxy | www.privacyview.com |

## Sharing files

Sharing files is a potentially risky activity that can be exploited by criminals to access your computer and get your personal information. However, there are a few protective measures you can implement to reduce the possibility of your personal information being stolen.

♦ **Keep your protection software up to date**
   Always ensure that your anti-spyware, anti-adware and anti-virus software is up to date and fully functional before installing a P2P program or exchanging any files.

♦ **Choose a recognised file sharing company which has fully developed their program**
   These are the companies who have released multiple

versions of their software to improve, update and eliminate any problems that earlier versions may have had. In addition, consider paying for a premium version that does not have any of the adware that is sometimes installed with free versions.

◆ **Only use trusted websites to download file sharing programs**
The best programs are those that are free from adware and spyware, that check for viruses and also offer a no-spyware guarantee.

◆ **Always disable the feature that allows users to browse your files directly**
This is a large security risk because hackers can exploit this feature to access your system directly.

### Downloading files

One of the main problems with using P2P programs is that you can never be too sure exactly what you are downloading. Users can save files with any name they choose which means that viruses or offensive material can be innocently disguised as the latest single or movie trailer. Providing your anti-virus program is kept up to date, any viruses should be detected and quarantined before they can do any damage. Offensive material is more difficult to detect because unless it contains a virus then you will not know there is a problem until it is viewed.

When software is downloaded, any executable (.exe) files must be treated with extreme caution because they may contain a virus or spyware that is activated when the file is opened. To reduce this risk, never click on Run when downloading a file because this will bypass your anti-virus software. Instead, select Save because at least your anti-virus software will be able to detect any potential problems. As an extra precautionary measure, only download software directly from the manufacturer or from trusted download websites instead of from P2P programs. The following sites are very useful.

www.computeractive.co.uk
www.download.com
www.pcworld.com
www.tucows.com
www.zdnet.com

Similarly, music files can also be safely downloaded from paid-for sites such as:

www.7digital.com
www.hmvdigital.com
www.napster.co.uk
www.tescodownloads.com
www.apple.com/itunes

## ERASING YOUR HARD DRIVE

The more often you use your computer the more personal and sensitive data it will contain. This can be a problem if you want to sell, donate, trade-in or dispose of your computer because your personal information can be retrieved easily and used by thieves, criminals and fraudsters. Many people think that simply deleting files or reformatting their hard drive is sufficient to destroy the data it contains and render it illegible but this is not the case.

When computer files are deleted they are not completely removed from the hard drive. Instead, only the first part of the file name is removed and the file becomes hidden. The information contained within the file will remain intact until it is overwritten. This means that your data can be easily retrieved with one of the many data-recovery tools that are freely available. These programs are ideal if your computer crashes and you need to recover and restore your lost files but they can also be used by criminals to uncover your personal information.

One rather drastic solution is to remove your hard drive and destroy it with a hammer, or by burning or drilling holes through it. You could also use a process called 'degaussing' which uses a strong magnetic field to remove the information safely. This is a relatively expensive process and is usually only used by companies and government organisations to destroy highly sensitive data. Completely destroying a hard drive seems such a waste when it could be donated to charity. Nevertheless, it is important to ensure that your personal information is not recoverable. This can be done by using a specialised utility program to erase the information from your drive.

### Data-wiping programs
Data-wiping programs, which are also known as file shredders, are not designed to wipe your drive in the traditional sense by removing your data. Instead, they overwrite your information with a combination of zeros and random number patterns, which renders your data unreadable even with sophisticated data restoration

programs. A quick internet search will reveal that many data removal programs are available, these include:

| | |
|---|---|
| BCWipe | www.jetico.com |
| Blancco Data Cleaner | www.blancco.com |
| Darik's Boot and Nuke | http://dban.sourceforge.net |
| Ontrack Data Eraser | www.ontrack.com |
| Eraser | www.heidi.ie |
| Eraseyourharddrive.com | www.eraseyourharddrive.com |
| KillDisk | www.killdisk.com |
| Norton Wipe | www.symantec.com |
| R-Wipe & Clean | www.r-wipe.com |
| ShredIt | www.mireth.com |
| Secure-Delete | www.secure-delete.net |

Some of these programs are available as a free or trial download while others are only available to buy. The free and trial versions will have limited functionality whereas the bought programs will have a wider range of features.

### Using data-wiping programs

When wiping your drive it is important to wipe the entire drive and not just the files that you consider are sensitive. This is because when files and documents are created, some systems automatically save back-up copies to temporary folders or unused parts of your drive. These files can be easily recovered with data-recovery programs or even simple MS-DOS commands such as 'undelete', so it is important to ensure that they are no longer accessible. After using a shredder for the first time, check how secure the program is by using a data-recovery tool to try to restore any files that have been shredded.

## Choosing a file shredder

When choosing a file shredder, look for a program with the flexibility to shred specific files and folders such as the recycle bin and temporary files in addition to an entire hard drive. Other useful features include:

- **Safe place folder**

  A secure folder will be created for any files and folders that you do not want to accidentally shred. For security reasons, it is advisable to avoid using this for sensitive documents because this obviously defeats the purpose of the shredder.

- **Shred all free space**

  This will clean up your computing history, including internet activity, cookies, Instant Messenger chat history and other temporary internet files.

- **Shred system files**

  With this feature, temporary system files, old deleted files and temporary program files including automatically saved previous file versions will be shredded.

- **Numbers of passes**

  Some shredders offer multiple wipe options to overwrite information but there is some debate whether this is necessary. Although it may be possible to recover information that has been overwritten a number of times, the equipment required is extremely expensive and not very common. For most systems one wipe will be sufficient but if your data is particularly sensitive then more than one pass is a worthwhile feature.

- **Military and government approved security standards**
  These can include the UK Government Infosec Standard 5 (1 or 3 pass options), the United States Department of Defence 52202.22-M (7 passes) or the Gutmann Algorithm (35 passes). Some programs will also generate a security certificate at the end of the process stating that your computer has been wiped to a particular standard.

## TOP TEN TIPS TO KEEP YOUR COMPUTER SECURE

✔ Always keep your operating system updated by downloading the latest security patches directly from the manufacturer's website.

✔ Install and use a comprehensive internet security suite that includes a firewall, anti-virus, anti-spyware, spam protection and online identity theft blocking and ensure that it is always kept up to date. Run regular system scans to search for and remove spyware and viruses.

✔ Set your internet browser settings to the highest security protection level and always use a firewall to protect yourself and your computer from online threats.

✔ Create, protect and store, strong non-dictionary passwords that are difficult to crack. The strongest passwords are those that use the entire keyboard to create a random string of upper and lower case letters, numbers, keyboard symbols and punctuation marks.

✔ Password protect your system and screen saver to prevent unauthorised users from accessing your computer.

✔ Ensure your wireless network is as secure as possible by password protecting your router and setting your network to the highest encryption level that your equipment will support.

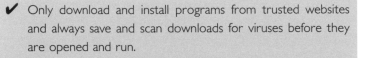

✔ Only download and install programs from trusted websites and always save and scan downloads for viruses before they are opened and run.

✔ Never open an email or attachment from an unknown source. Only download or read emails from trustworthy sources that you recognise and always ensure that attachments are scanned for viruses before they are opened.

✔ Always use a spam filter to protect your computer from unsolicited and unwanted spam emails.

✔ Turn off file sharing to prevent strangers from accessing your computer and always disconnect from the internet when you are not online.

## VICTIMS' STORIES

### Online identity theft

When Elliott's bank statement arrived he was shocked to discover that huge sums of money had been transferred from his bank account through a series of online transactions. Somebody had discovered his username and password and had effectively stolen his identity. One of the advantages with online banking is that after an online account is opened, the account holder can manage their account without ever needing to contact the bank. This can also be a disadvantage because, unless they are informed otherwise, the bank has no reason to suspect that an account is being accessed by anyone other than the account holder. This is why it is important to guard your username and password, use a strong password that is regularly changed and never access your account from a public computer.

Elliott immediately contacted his bank and arranged for his account to be temporarily suspended until the matter was fully resolved. The bank conducted a thorough investigation but this took a number of weeks to complete. During this time he was unable to access his account but fortunately he was able to borrow money from his family and friends. The bank finally refunded all of the money that had been stolen but the whole situation has made him more cautious when banking online.

### Financial identity fraud

Ben did not notice that his wallet had been stolen until he returned home from work. By this time his wife had already received a telephone call allegedly from the tax office, claiming that they had a rebate for him and they needed to confirm his address. She naively gave them their address and even corrected them when they got Ben's mother's maiden name wrong. Ben's wallet contained his driving licence together with every credit and debit card that he owned. He contacted his bank but it was too late, the criminals had used his debit card and driving licence to assume his identity and steal £4,500 over the counter from his bank. They also used his credit cards to buy £2,600 of electrical equipment and £1,280 of jewellery.

All of Ben's money was eventually returned but he no longer uses his mother's maiden name as a means of security. He also leaves his driving licence at home and only carries one credit and debit card in his wallet, the others are left safely at home for emergency use only.

# 4

# Using the Internet Safely

In recent years the growth of the internet has been phenomenal and as the cost of computing continues to decrease this trend looks set to continue. The internet has become such a large and important part of everyday life that it can sometimes be difficult to remember what life was like without it. For the majority of people, it has become an invaluable tool for shopping, banking, communicating and generally making life a little easier. Unfortunately, it has also created new opportunities for criminals and fraudsters to take advantage of unsuspecting users. Fortunately, there are a number of ways to reduce these risks provided that you are aware of the variety of methods that criminals and fraudsters use. This chapter will offer help and advice about how to identify potential threats and scams and how to shop, bank, communicate and download safely.

## TYPES OF INTERNET FRAUD

There are so many different types of internet fraud that to list and fully explain all of them would probably require the publication of another book. However, the majority of frauds are based on similar principles and practices so this book will highlight the most common types which include:

- spoof email and phishing scams
- advance fee and 419 fraud
- pharming
- lottery fraud
- online auction fraud
- fake online shop fraud.

The golden rule with any fraud is that if it looks too good to be true, then it probably is. Experienced criminals and fraudsters have spent many years perfecting their style and technique to find out what works and what does not. Any unsolicited opportunity to make money should always be regarded as a fraud because genuine opportunities do not need to be marketed in this way. Nevertheless, many unsuspecting people are regularly cheated out of their money and possessions which can lead to all kinds of other problems. The fortunate part of these scams is that, in order to work, they require action on your part to reply and divulge your details, so do not reply.

## Spoof email and phishing scams

This type of fraud uses spoof email and phishing scams to try to obtain your personal security information. This is a three-step process whereby fraudsters first send millions of random and unsolicited emails that appear to be from genuine online companies such as banks and shops. Fraudsters play the law of averages and trust that by sending so many emails they will eventually reach potential victims who have dealings with the company being targeted.

The exact content of the email will vary between fraudsters but the overall message will be the same. The email will claim that the company needs to confirm or update your personal details because they are making technical improvements to their systems. They will usually encourage you to reply immediately by claiming that you will no longer be able to access your account if you do not update your details. The second step of the process involves you clicking on the link provided by the email. This will take you to a security log-in page that appears to look genuine but has in fact been set up by the fraudster. The moment you enter your personal details then step three is complete; you have given the fraudster all they need to steal your money or your identity. This is an example of a typical phishing email:

Dear Any National Bank customer,

Any National Bank Customer Service requests you to complete our Online Banking Customer Form.

This procedure is obligatory for all internet banking users of Any National Bank and you will be unable to access your account until the form has been completed.

Please click the hyperlink below to access Online Banking Customer Form.

**http://update-749365.anynationalbank.com/ userdatadirectory/start.aspx**

Please do not respond to this email.

Copyright 20XX. Any National Bank plc. All Rights Reserved.

*Be suspicious*

Whenever you receive an email asking for any personal details, always be suspicious and remember that a genuine company will never ask for information in this way. Your bank might ask you to confirm particular characters from your password but never the entire password. If you do receive a suspicious looking email or you are unsure if it is genuine then always contact the sending company first before divulging any personal details. Also be wary of links contained in emails because you never know where they will take you. A security log-in page can appear to look genuine at first but unless the http changes to https in the Internet address bar and a locked padlock or unbroken chain can be seen inside your web browser then do not proceed.

*Reporting email scams*

There are so many different types of email scams that keeping up with them all can be quite difficult. To help with this, organisations including Bank Safe Online and Miller Smiles have created a large archive of these emails and actively encourage users to forward others to them. To do this, simply create a new email message, drag and drop the original scam email into the new email as a file attachment and send it to:

Bank Safe Online          www.banksafeonline.org.uk
                  Email: reports@banksafeonline.org.uk

Miller Smiles              www.millersmiles.co.uk
                  Email: spoof@millersmiles.co.uk

Further advice and information about identifying and dealing with these scams can be obtained from:

Anti-Phishing Working Group     www.antiphishing.org
Fraud Watch International
                    www.fraudwatchinternational.com
Get Safe Online             www.getsafeonline.org.uk
Spamfo                   www.spamfo.co.uk

## Advance fee and 419 frauds

These are a type of spam that uses phishing as a means to contact millions of potential victims. Although these scams are all executed slightly differently, their underlying principles are the same. They work by notifying you that you have won a lottery, inherited some money or your bank account is needed to transfer huge sums of money from a foreign country. You will usually be asked to provide your bank details, confirm your identity with a passport or driving licence and pay an advance fee to cover taxes, transfer fees and other similar non-existent charges. When the transaction is complete the advance fee you have paid will go directly to the fraudster and you will never hear from them again.

The 419 frauds are a little more complicated but they work in a similar way. They are named after the section of the Nigerian Criminal Code where the majority of these frauds originate. The email will claim to be from a high-ranking foreign government or bank official who needs your bank account to transfer a huge sum of money from their country. In exchange for your assistance you will be able to keep a proportion of the money which is usually about a third. The 'official' will explain how they are able to access surplus or unclaimed funds from over-invoiced projects, completed contracts or from a previous political regime. You will probably be informed that you have been recommended by a business associate because of your integrity and at this point the importance of secrecy will be stressed because the money would be seized if corrupt government officials knew of its existence.

As the fraud progresses you will be asked to pay a variety of advance fees. These will usually start comparatively small against the money you have been promised but they will gradually increase as the money is about to be transferred. A variety of reasons will be given for these including bribing government officials, legal expenses, customs clearance, local taxes and bank charges. Fraudsters have become highly experienced at executing this type of fraud and will often assure potential victims with official looking documents or they will operate an untraceable satellite phone that will appear to be answered by a government department. An example of a typical advance fee fraud email is shown on page 120.

### Pharming

Pharming is another form of fraud that involves redirecting internet traffic but unlike phishing no emails are used. Instead, criminals gain access to a genuine company's website and reprogram their internet address to an identical cloned site that they have set up. This means that even though the correct address has been typed into your web browser you are automatically directed to the fraudster's website without even realising. When you attempt to log-in at this site your personal details and password will be captured and used by fraudsters to access your account. Although this type of

Nigerian National Petroleum Corporation (NNPC)
NNPC Towers
Central Area
Abuja
Nigeria

FROM THE DESK OF MR COLE JOSEPH
47 HILTON AVENUE
VICTORIA ISLAND
LAGOS, NIGERIA

Dear Friend,

I am a director in the foreign affairs department of the Nigerian National Petroleum Corporation (NNPC). I got your email during a personal research on the internet and wish to use this opportunity to notify you of the existence of a certain amount we wish to transfer overseas for the purpose of investments and importation of goods from your country.

In May 20XX, a contract of 66 million United States dollars ($66,000,000) was awarded to a foreign company by my ministry. The contract was supply, erection and system optimisation of super polyore 200,000-bpsd, system optimisation of 280,000-monax axial plants and the computerisation of conveyor belt for Kaduna refinery. With only the consent of the head of the contract evaluation department, I over invoiced the contract value by thirty-four million United States dollars ($34,000,000).

The contract has been completed long ago and the foreign company fully paid off. But in the office files and paper work, the company is still owed USD34M representing the over invoiced amount. Because this amount is derived from the award and execution of a foreign contract, there is no way the money can be paid locally. That is why I contacted you so that we can do the project together for our mutual benefit. We have concluded every necessary arrangement to transfer this amount to a foreign account as the final phase payment for the said contract. What we need is your bank account into which we can deposit the money and after we shall come over there to share the money with you.

We sincerely need an honest person to work with and have agreed to share the money in the following percentages, 70% will be for us who will effect the transfer and 30% will be for you whose account is used to secure the funds. There is no risk involvement because applications will be made to the concerned Federal ministries and with official approvals given by the Federal government before the Central Bank of Nigeria will be officially empowered to wire the funds to your account by telegraphic transfer.

If you are interested, send your reply through my direct and private email address (xxxxxxxxxx@xxxxx.xxx) indicating your full names or company name and address and your direct telephone and fax numbers for effective communication that this transaction needs. Do not reply through the Nigerian National Petroleum Corporation email address because it belongs to the senior staffs for public use. I will also need the name and address of the bank you will like us to deposit the money, the telephone and fax numbers of the bank, your account number etc. Everything has been arranged and I will send more information about the business transaction to you as soon as I hear from you. For obvious reasons, please keep the proposal top secret and highly confidential.

Kind regards,

Cole

fraud is technically possible, the good news is that to date there have not been any reported cases.

### Lottery fraud

There are numerous variations of these frauds but they all follow a similar pattern. In the first instance, millions of people are notified that they have won an overseas lottery. This originally happened by post but phishing is now more commonly used. To attract your attention, the first email will probably ask you to respond within a short period of time and will initially refrain from mentioning that a small fee will be required to release your winnings. This fee will often be disguised as a charge to cover processing, handling, postage, registration, insurance, bank charges or other similar costs.

You will also be advised to reply to a claims agent who can be contacted on a premium rate phone line, which is likely to be part of the scam, or through an untraceable email address. When contact is made, you will be asked to divulge as much personal information as possible and you may even be required to confirm your identity with a driving licence or passport. At this stage, the fraudster will have acquired sufficient information to steal or clone your identity.

The next step will be an email from the claims agent with three collection options which all require an advance fee payment.

1. **Your winnings, less a handling fee, can be transferred directly to your bank account**
   This will probably be the first time that an advance fee payment will be mentioned.

2. **To avoid paying a handling fee, you can choose to open an online account at a specified bank**
This will invariably be a fake bank that will require an initial deposit to open the account. Note that the handling fee has been replaced by a deposit which is effectively the same.

3. **You can also choose to collect your winnings personally**
This will invariably involve travelling to a foreign country which, in recent years, has often been Amsterdam. You will be required to pay a release fee and your winnings will be paid with counterfeit currency.

To help create the illusion that you have actually won some money and to persuade you to respond, the fraudster may even send you a cheque that will allegedly clear as soon as your personal details have been confirmed. Unfortunately, this cheque will either be counterfeit or stolen and will definitely be refused by the bank. As the fraud is played out your personal details will either be sold to other fraudsters or your bank account will be cleared of funds. An example of a typical lottery fraud email is shown opposite.

**Online auction fraud**
This type of fraud involves high priced goods such as laptops, mobile phones, digital cameras, laser printers, computer scanners, televisions, video games consoles or digital video cameras being offered at very low prices. There are two main ways that the scam works: you either pay for goods that never arrive or you pay for brand new

NATIONAL EURO LOTTERY
BIJLMERDREEF 657
1102 BS AMSTERDAM
THE NETHERLANDS

FROM:   THE PROMOTIONAL SECRETARY
        INTERNATIONAL PROMOTIONS/PRIZE AWARD DEPARTMENT

## ATTENTION

After a successful completion of the 2nd category draws of NATIONAL EURO LOTTERY, held on 24th November 20xx, we are pleased to inform you of the official announcement today, that you have emerged one of the winners of the NATIONAL EURO LOTTERY INTERNATIONAL PROGRAMS, which is part of our promotional draws.

Participants were selected through a computer ballot system drawn from 25,000 names/email addresses of individuals and companies from Africa, America, Asia, Australia, Canada, Europe, Middle East, and New Zealand as part of our International Promotions Program.

You are attached to ticket number N.E.L. 714-5-9827, drew the lucky numbers N.E.L .03- 15- 23- 25- 35- 40 and consequently won in the 2nd Category.

You have therefore been awarded a lump sum pay out of US$1,000,000.00 (one million United States dollars) which is the winning payout for 2nd category winners. This is from the total prize money of US$5,700,000.00 shared among the three international winners in the 2nd category.

## CONGRATULATIONS!

Your fund is now deposited with a financial institution with REFERENCE NUMBER: N.E.L A718-3 and BATCH NUMBER: 224-DA, insured on your name. To avoid mix up of numbers and names, we request that you keep this award strictly from public notice until the entire process of transferring your claim has been completed, and your funds remitted to your account. This is part of our security protocol to avoid double claiming or unscrupulous acts by participants of this program.

We also wish to bring to your notice our end of year (20xx) high stakes where you stand a chance of winning up to US$1.3 billion; we hope that with a part of your prize you will participate.

Please contact your claims agent immediately, to begin your claims process;

Mr Xxxxxxx Xxxx
FOREIGN SERVICE MANAGER,
NATIONAL EURO LOTTERY
EMAIL: xxxxxxxxx@xxxxxxxx.xxx
PHONE: xxx xxx xxx xxx

For due processing and remittance of your prize money to a designated account of your choice. Remember, all winnings must be claimed not later than 20th Dec 20xx.

## NOTE:

To avoid unnecessary delays and complications, please remember to quote your reference and batch numbers provided above, in your correspondence with your claims agent.

Congratulations once again from all our staff and thank you for being part of our promotions program.

Yours sincerely,

Xxxxxx Xxxxxx
PROMOTIONAL SECRETARY

goods but only receive second-hand or similar goods of a lower value. The fraudster will either advertise the item using a genuine auction account with good feedback that they have stolen or they will make direct contact by email after you have bid for a similar item.

To take advantage of these prices, which can be as low as a third of their full retail price, you will be asked to contact the seller away from the auction company. This will usually be through a free disposable email account that the fraudster will discard soon afterwards. The fraudster will try to be as persuasive as possible to gain your confidence and convince you to buy from them. They will stress the importance of their honesty and may even provide a shipping number for the goods. Unfortunately, this will either be a false number, an empty box or goods of far less value than those you have paid for.

Whenever you deal with sellers in this way, it is important to remember that you are no longer protected by the auction company when things go wrong. When contact is made they will usually explain how they can only accept payment through Western Union because of problems they have experienced with other money transfer companies. Western Union have unfortunately become synonymous with online auction fraud but it must be stressed that there is nothing wrong with Western Union as a money transfer provider. In fact they offer a very good service. The problem is that their service is not intended for online purchases from unknown online sellers and this is categorically stated in their terms and conditions.

### Fake online shop fraud

This involves setting up a fake online shop offering popular high priced goods at incredibly low prices. These will usually be electronic goods including computers, digital cameras, televisions, mobile phones, games consoles and digital video cameras that fraudsters know will attract plenty of potential customers. The fraud works by the fraudsters claiming that they are regrettably unable to accept traditional methods of payment such as credit or debit cards, postal orders, cheques or bank transfers. Instead they will insist that payment is only made through untraceable companies such as Western Union or Moneygram. The buyer pays for goods that never arrive and because of the way that payment is made they are unable to recover their money.

## USING ONLINE USERNAMES AND PASSWORDS

There was a time when online usernames and passwords were only required to access secure websites but they are now being increasingly used for other websites. For example, whenever you buy from an online retailer you will usually be asked to set up a customer account complete with a username and password. To do this, some companies will only require your email address whereas others may also request your home address or other personal information. The purpose of these customer accounts is twofold. Firstly, the online company can create a database of interested customers whom they can contact with special offers or new products providing the customer has not declined to receive direct mailings. Secondly, the customer is able to reorder from the site without having to re-enter all of their personal details.

Providing that you are satisfied with their Privacy Policy (see page 137, Using Secure Websites), this is a perfectly acceptable form of marketing. Some companies will not allow access to their website until your details have been registered. The company will then use your details to keep you informed of promotional offers or new products. Under the terms of the Data Protection Act you should always be given the opportunity to decline receiving marketing information in this way.

### Choosing a password

The more often you access websites that require passwords and usernames the more information you will have to remember. This might tempt you to register the same log-in details with a number of different websites but from a security point of view this should always be avoided. If a fraudster discovers your log-in details to one account then they can potentially access all of your accounts. Whenever you are online always keep your passwords and PINs safe. This is particularly important if you are accessing the internet in a public place where people can see what you are typing. For further information, see page 67, Using Passwords.

## SHOPPING ONLINE

The phenomenal growth of the internet has seen millions of new companies opening for business. With comparatively low overheads and the potential to attract customers from all over the world, internet companies can become very successful very quickly. Companies such as Amazon, Ebay, Play.com, CD Wow and Firebox have all shown that competitive prices and good customer service make for a winning combination.

However, it's not just new companies that are doing well, the majority of high street retailers have embraced the internet by setting up online versions of their stores. Whereas the internet used to offer a competitive alternative to high street shopping, many companies have realised that it can also be used as an extension to their traditional business. But with so many different companies to choose from it can often be difficult to decide which ones are the best. A well-designed website can easily create the impression of a large, established company but the reality can sometimes be quite different. A website should never be judged solely by its look. So, how do you know which sites to trust?

### Using trustworthy websites

A good place to start is with large reputable high street names that you recognise such as Argos, Boots, Comet, Currys, Dixons, HMV, PC World, Waterstones, Woolworths or WH Smith. These companies will often sell goods at Internet Exclusive prices which are considerably cheaper than those available in their stores. However, not all internet companies have a high street presence but they can still offer the same standards of customer service. The key is to check that the website and the retailer are genuine by looking for their physical address and telephone number. Websites that do not provide any contact details or only use a PO Box address or a mobile telephone number should generally be avoided.

In the interest of good customer relations, genuine companies will prominently display their contact details and actively encourage feedback from their online visitors.

In addition, personal recommendations, magazine reviews and independent comparison websites are also good ways to find out about reputable companies, these sites include:

www.comparebuyandsave.com
www.compareprices.co.uk
www.dooyoo.co.uk
www.kelkoo.co.uk
www.moneysupermarket.com
www.pricechecker.co.uk
www.pricerunner.co.uk
www.shopsafe.co.uk
www.shopzilla.co.uk

While visiting websites, take care when typing the company name into your browser's address bar because fraudsters have been known to set up websites with similarly spelt names to attract some internet traffic. These fraudulent sites will resemble genuine websites but any information submitted to them will be used by the fraudster to steal from you.

## Using credit cards

If you frequently use the internet to shop online then you might want to consider opening a separate, internet-only credit card account. Credit cards offer a variety of additional benefits that are not available when you pay by cash or cheque. These include:

♦ **Purchase insurance** – some cards will insure your purchases for up to 90 days against lost, stolen or faulty goods.

- **Identity theft assistance** – if your card and personal details are used to fraudulently buy goods or services then the card company will help to resolve the situation.

- **Free insurance** – if you pay for a holiday or buy airline tickets with your card then most companies will include free travel insurance with your purchase but always check the terms and conditions of the policy to ensure they meet your requirements.

- **Loss protection** – if your card becomes lost or stolen then you will not be liable for any purchases provided that you immediately notify your card provider.

Using a single internet-only card will also allow you to easily keep track of your online purchases. Whenever you receive a statement, always check it thoroughly and immediately report any unauthorised transactions to your card company. Although statements are usually sent on a monthly basis, practically all card companies now allow cardholders to access their account online. This means that you can regularly check your account to ensure that your card has not been fraudulently used.

### Sign up for extra credit card security

Credit card companies have taken a proactive approach to internet fraud by developing additional security measures to protect you when shopping online. Both MasterCard and Visa have developed secure online password pro-tected identity checking systems that cardholders can sign up for. The MasterCard SecureCode and Verified by Visa systems work by enabling you to register an additional password to your card. This password will then be required by participating websites when making a purchase with your card.

This means that even if your card is lost or stolen it cannot be used without knowing your password. You will often be given the opportunity to sign up for these schemes when you reach the payment section at participating sites. Alternatively, you can either contact the companies direct or visit Shop Safe Online which provides information about registering and using the systems.

| | |
|---|---|
| MasterCard SecureCode | www.mastercard.com |
| Verified by Visa | www.visaeurope.com |
| Shop Safe Online | www.shopsafeonline.org.uk |

**Print your order**
Whenever you buy online always print a copy of your order. Most retailers will automatically send a receipt together with a copy of your order to your designated email address, but it is also worth printing your order directly from the screen when the transaction is complete. You should also print copies of the retailer's terms and conditions, their delivery conditions and their returns policy. These will prove extremely useful in the event of any problems arising with your purchase. This is particularly important when dealing with international companies because the more information you have, the greater your chance of resolving any issues. In some cases, your bank or building society may be able to intervene on your behalf but they can only do this if they have access to all the relevant information.

## Using online auctions

Online auctions can be a great way to get a bargain and save a lot of money, or sell goods and make money, but they can also be used by fraudsters to scam unsuspecting users. However, if you are careful and you follow the rules then they can also be a lot of fun. Online auctions work in a similar way to traditional auctions whereby a seller offers an item for sale and then buyers bid against each other until the auction closes and the highest bidder wins. Most auctions often start with a comparatively low opening price to entice buyers to start bidding. Some popular online auction websites include:

| | |
|---|---|
| Auction Auto Trader | www.auctionautotrader.com |
| Amazon Auctions | http://s1.amazon.co.uk |
| Ebay | www.ebay.co.uk |
| CQout | www.cqout.com |
| QXL | www.qxl.co.uk |
| Virgin Wines Auctions | www.virginwines.com |

Alternatively, a comprehensive list of other online auctions can be obtained from:

| | |
|---|---|
| Auction Lot Watch | www.auctionlotwatch.co.uk |

Auctions usually last between one and ten days but some auction companies offer longer periods. Sometimes the seller will set an undisclosed reserve price that the item must reach before it can be sold. If there is not a reserve price then the item will be sold to the highest bidder at the close of the auction. If online auctions are new to you, then it is worth reading through the getting started guides provided by the auction company. These will give you a good understanding about how the system works, what you can and cannot sell, what the rules and regulations are and what the company can and cannot do if something goes wrong.

## Getting started

Before you can start buying or selling at an auction you will need to open an account with the auction company. This will involve creating a log-in name and setting a password. You will also be asked to confirm your identity, which is usually done by registering a credit or debit card with the company. This is a perfectly legitimate process and the company will never charge anything to your account without your permission. To help protect your identity, your log-in name should be different from your email address and as always, your password should be a combination of numbers and letters in both upper and lower case. (For further information, see page 67, Using Passwords.) Once you have opened an account you can buy or sell as many items as you want.

## Trading safely

Although the vast majority of auctions abide by the rules and operate without problem, there will always be a small percentage that are not quite what they seem. Auction companies are keen to protect their users and will endeavour to remove any potentially fraudulent or illegal auctions before their users can be taken advantage of.

Nevertheless, some auctions inevitably slip through the net but there are a number of preventive steps you can take to help ensure that you are not the victim of a scam.

As a buyer, make sure that you only buy from reputable sellers by looking through their profile, checking their rating and examining their transaction history. This will give you a good idea about the type of seller you are dealing with. For example, sellers with lots of negative feedback should always be avoided but sellers with a low rating are not necessarily bad, they are perhaps just new to selling.

You could also question the seller by email and gauge their response. Prompt, courteous replies naturally create a far better impression than slow or offensive ones. Useful questions include confirmation of postage costs, delivery times and acceptable methods of payment. The seller's location is also important because overseas sellers can be difficult to chase if something goes wrong. Similarly, if the seller is a business then try to confirm that they are genuine by telephoning or visiting them. As a potential buyer it is your responsibility to validate the integrity of the seller by exercising caution and using your judgement.

When you are selling goods always be as truthful as possible and always include a genuine photograph. These can usually be uploaded for free and will enable potential bidders to see exactly what they are buying. As a seller, never be tempted to accept a low price or close an auction early, because the best bids often come just as the auction is about to finish. After the auction ends you will need to exchange a few personal details with the buyer or seller such as a delivery address. Always be wary when sharing personal information and never give out more information that you need to.

## Using PayPal

PayPal is an electronic payment service that is widely recognised as a safe and immediate way to exchange money. You do not need to have a PayPal account to pay with PayPal for an auction but you will need an account to accept PayPal payments. Opening an account is a free and relatively simple process, which involves confirming your identity with a credit or debit card and assigning a bank account to receive payments. When a buyer uses PayPal to pay for an auction, the total purchase price is paid to PayPal which then credits the buyer's account less a small processing fee. As soon as the transaction is complete, both the buyer and the seller are notified. The seller is then able to send the goods safe in the knowledge that payment has been received. If there is a problem with the auction such as the goods not arriving or not being as described then, after investigation, PayPal are usually able to reimburse the buyer in full.

## Common online auction scams

Always exercise caution if you see a price that appears too good to be true because it probably is. Sometimes a seller will appear to be offering a genuine product at a great price but after you have paid your money, the goods will either never arrive or will turn out to be counterfeit. Conversely, a buyer might try to persuade you to send off an item before they have paid for it by promising to pay a higher price when they receive it. This will be a scam and you will never see your money, so always ensure that you receive payment before sending anything off.

As with banks and other financial institutions, auction companies are frequently targeted by fraudsters with phishing emails. If you ever receive an email asking you to click on a link to update your personal details then do not respond. These emails are sent in their millions to persuade unsuspecting users to disclose passwords and other security information which the fraudster uses to compromise your account. If you think that your account has been fraudulently used, then immediately report this to the auction company.

### Resolving problems

If you experience any problems when buying or selling at an auction then report these to the auction company. They will usually ask to see copies of all correspondence that has been exchanged so always keep these safe. In some cases, a breakdown in communication can occur when emails get blocked by spam filters so remember to check your spam folder regularly. Whenever possible, the auction company will endeavour to resolve any genuine problems on your behalf.

## BANKING ONLINE

With the opportunity to access your account at any time of the day or night, online banking has become an extremely popular way to organise your finances and help make life a little easier. Millions of people regularly bank online and as the cost of computing continues to become less expensive, millions more will follow. Despite these huge numbers, the risk of becoming a victim to banking fraud is extremely low. Banks need to ensure that their systems are completely secure so they are constantly developing new ways to protect themselves from hackers, which has meant that their systems are incredibly difficult to access.

Therefore, criminals will use any means of deception in an attempt to get information directly from you that can be used to access your account. The most common way to do this is through phishing which involves sending millions of random emails that appear to be from genuine banks or organisations. The emails usually claim that it is necessary to update your personal security information by following a link that they helpfully provide. Unfortunately, this only leads to fake websites that the fraudsters have set up to capture your personal details. For further information, see page 114, Types of Internet Fraud.

Trojans are another method that criminals can use to access your computer and personal details. They are types of computer viruses that, once installed, quietly run in the background so that you are unaware they are even there. Some Trojans delete and scramble files while others can create a log of your keystrokes that criminals can use to see your passwords and other personal information. To reduce the possibility of accidentally allowing a Trojan to install itself on your computer, ensure that your system has up-to-date anti-virus software and a firewall installed. For more information see Chapter 3, Keeping Your Computer Secure.

### Banking safely
The first rule of online banking is to ensure that you only ever contact your bank directly. Never, under any circumstances, follow a link from an email or another website. Although many trusted companies send genuine links in this way, fraudsters can easily create genuine-looking websites that can be used to capture your log-in

details. Although these sites are generally closed down relatively quickly, fraudsters can get thousands of account details in the short time they are accessible. It is worth remembering that your bank will never ask for information in this way, so never disclose any personal security details to anyone you do not trust. If you do need to update your details then this should be done by directly entering their internet address into your browser to access your account.

In order to access your bank account, you will be required to set up a password and PIN. Sometimes your bank might provide an initial password and PIN that can be changed after you log-in. With so many different passwords to remember it can be tempting to use the same passwords for all of your accounts. This should be avoided because if a fraudster discovers your password they will be able to access all of your accounts. For more information about creating, storing and protecting passwords, see page 67, Using Passwords. Further advice and guidance about online banking fraud protection is available from the security section of your bank's website and also from Bank Safe Online at www.banksafeon line.org.uk

## USING SECURE WEBSITES

Shopping and banking from a computer can sometimes create a false sense of security but you still need to remain vigilant. The first step is to ensure that you only use websites that have a secure server connection. These are used to encrypt your personal information before it is sent online, which means that it cannot be intercepted and read by fraudsters. Banks and financial companies always use secure servers but this does not apply to all online retailers. Websites that do not have a secure server will usually allow customers to pay over the telephone or to send payment by post. While the majority of these will be genuine companies offering genuine goods or services, always exercise caution when dealing with these companies. There are two ways to tell if a website is secure.

1. **Check the security icon on your computer screen**
   Depending on your browser this will either be a locked padlock or an unbroken key. If you are using Internet Explorer 7 or Firefox 2 then the locked padlock will usually be found at the top of the screen. Either of these icons mean that the website is secure but if you have followed a link from another source, then always re-type the company name directly into the address bar. Fraudsters have been known to set up fake websites with a genuine-looking security icon pasted onto the page.

2. **Check that a secure server is being used**
   Look at the http at the beginning of the company's internet address, this will automatically change to https when a secure connection is used to make a purchase. In some internet browsers, the address bar may also change to green which means that the website has an additional level of security.

## Logging out

When you have finished using a secure server it is important that you log out from the website because if you do not then it is possible that your financial details may be read by others. This is particularly important if you are using a public or work computer that other people have access to. In most cases, secure servers will not allow users to revisit pages by simply clicking on the back button without resending the information. Sometimes, however, the page can remain in the computer's memory and can still be accessed through the history tab.

## Privacy policies

As an additional security measure and particularly before using a new or unknown website, always check the company's privacy policy to see how your personal information will be secured, handled and stored. The privacy policy should also provide details about how to contact the company and how personal information can be sent without using the internet.

The majority of companies share customer information with other organisations but under the terms of the Data Protection Act, you must always be given the opportunity to decline sharing your details. When submitting your personal details, most websites will provide a tick box for you to agree or disagree for your information to be shared. The golden rule to remember is that if you have any concerns or reservations about submitting your personal information then do not send it.

## TOP TEN TIPS FOR USING THE INTERNET SAFELY

✔ Never click on links contained in unsolicited emails because you cannot guarantee exactly where these will take you.

✔ Only use a computer that you know is secure and never use a public computer to access any personal, confidential or sensitive data.

✔ Beware of phishing and other online threats and always remain vigilant against them.

✔ Only shop at secure and trusted websites by looking for the security icon which will either be a locked padlock or an unbroken key. Also check that the beginning of the company's Internet address changes from http to https which means that the connection is encrypted and secure. In some Internet browsers, the address bar may also change to green which means that the website has an additional level of security.

✔ Check that the website operates a privacy policy that you are comfortable with, print the policy and also print their terms and conditions together with a copy of any orders that you make.

✔ Never disclose personal information in chat rooms, forums or any social networking sites because these details can be fraudulently used against you.

✔ Consider using an internet-only credit card for online purchases. This will make checking your internet purchases easier and will reduce the chance of your card details being stolen.

✔ Sign up for MasterCard SecureCode or Verified by Visa to protect your online purchases with an additional password during the checkout process.

✔ Disable the auto complete function and uncheck the Remember My Details box.

✔ Always use a disposable email address when surfing the internet and choose an obscure name that will be difficult for spammers to guess.

## Victims' Stories

### Online auction identity fraud

Even though Kelly had never bought or sold goods at an online auction, her identity had still been used to fraudulently sell jewellery. The identity theft only came to light when Kelly received a threatening letter from an American law firm instructing her to refund their client £450 for a necklace that had been bought in good faith but was in fact counterfeit. The client had appointed the law firm after claiming to have contacted Kelly on numerous occasions and demanding a full refund but without success. The letter referred to specific emails and letters that were alleged to have been exchanged between Kelly and their client.

Kelly contacted the law firm but they were reluctant to believe that she was not involved with selling counterfeit jewellery. She also contacted the auction company but because she did not have an account with them they were not very helpful. Eventually, she was able to prove that she was elsewhere when some of the correspondence was exchanged and the law firm accepted that she had nothing to do with the jewellery. The matter is now being dealt with by the online auction company who have since closed the account and apologised for the inconvenience caused.

### Financial identity fraud (bin raiding)

When Lewis ripped up and threw away his old bank statements, it did not occur to him that they could be used to steal his money but that is exactly what happened. Three weeks later he discovered that £7,000 had been transferred from his account after criminals initially contacted his bank and arranged for his mailing address to be changed. They also arranged for a new debit card and PIN number to be sent to the new address so they could withdraw money from cash machines. Fortunately, Lewis noticed the withdrawals and immediately reported it to the bank which investigated and returned his money after three weeks.

Three months later Lewis was contacted by another bank who had received an application to open an online account in his name. Although the application was refused because a different address was on the form, this shows that once criminals have got someone's bank details they will continue using them until they have fully exhausted every avenue. Lewis now uses a shredder for any letters, statements and documents that have his name and address on. He also monitors his accounts on a daily basis and regularly checks his credit report to see if any unknown searches have been made.

# ⑤

# Identifying if You Are a Victim

As identity fraud continues to increase, it is more important than ever to remain vigilant and to be able to identify immediately if you become, or are at risk of becoming, a victim. This can be a difficult task because, by their very nature, identity fraudsters need to remain undetected for as long as possible. However, there are a variety of circumstances and situations which could increase the chance of your becoming a victim. These include:

- lost or stolen personal documents
- the disappearance of mail
- irregular and unauthorised transactions
- if your credit rating has been reduced.

## LOST OR STOLEN PERSONAL DOCUMENTS
If any of your personal documents become lost or stolen then you are more susceptible to identity fraud. As discussed in Keeping Your Personal Documents Secure, see page 44, these documents include your passport, birth certificate, driving licence, marriage certificate, share certificates, vehicle registration document, insurance documents and utility bills. A fraudster only needs a few details from some of these documents to assume your identity and steal from you, so it is important to ensure

they are always kept safe and secure. The best way to do this is to use a combination of a secure cabinet, a lockable drawer and a home safe to store them and never to carry more personal documents than are absolutely necessary.

## DISAPPEARANCE OF MAIL

If you suspect that your post has been compromised in any way, then you must report this to Royal Mail Customer Care on 0845 774 0740. They will be able to advise you if a mail redirection has been set up on your address without your knowledge. You will also be able to report the theft or loss of mail but before you can do this you need to be sure that your post has been sent. For example, bank statements, credit card statements and utility bills are routinely sent on specific dates but do you know when these are due? It is a good idea to keep a separate note of when these are expected so that you will immediately be aware of any problems.

If you share a communal letterbox, then the possibility of post becoming lost or stolen is greatly increased. To reduce this, there are a few preventive measures you can take. For example, try to collect your mail as soon after it has been delivered as possible. In most cases this will not always possible, so it may be worth installing a separate lockable letterbox to safely secure your post. These are relatively inexpensive but are worth every penny for the peace of mind they provide. Alternatively, consider renting a **PO** Box or arranging to have your post held at your local delivery office for you to collect. For further information, contact the Royal Mail Sales Centre on 0845 795 0950.

## IRREGULAR AND UNAUTHORISED TRANSACTIONS

As previously discussed, identity fraud victims will often remain unaware that they have been targeted until they receive a bill, invoice or receipt for goods or services that they have not purchased. Therefore, it is important to regularly check your bank or credit card statements for any irregular and unauthorised transactions that you do not recognise. Fortunately, the advent of online access to bank and credit card accounts means that these can be checked on a daily basis without the need to wait for a monthly statement to arrive. This also means that you can identify and potentially rectify any problems before they become serious issues that may affect your identity or your credit rating.

## YOUR CREDIT RATING HAS BEEN REDUCED

Your credit rating is one of the most important pieces of personal information you have because without it you will be unable to get credit cards, loans or mortgages. When your identity has been compromised, fraudsters will often use your personal details to apply for credit that they have no intention of repaying. This will obviously affect your credit rating but in most cases you will not realise this has happened until you receive letters from solicitors or debt collectors for debts that are not yours. Alternatively, you may also be refused credit despite having a good credit rating. The best way to check this is to obtain a copy of your credit report.

### Obtaining your credit report

Your credit report contains a detailed account of your

credit history including your repayments and previous credit applications. They also include any searches made by credit reference agencies to determine your credit rating, which can be useful if you do not recognise their origin. Your credit report can be obtained from one the three main credit reference agencies:

Callcredit
One Park Lane, Leeds, LS3 1EP
Automated Helpline: 0870 060 1414
Tel: 0113 244 1555
Fax: 0113 234 0050
www.callcredit.co.uk

Equifax
Credit File Advice Centre, PO Box 1140, Bradford, BD1 5US
Tel: 0870 010 0583
www.equifax.co.uk

Experian
Consumer Help Service, PO Box 9000, Nottingham, NG80 7WP
Tel: 0870 241 6212
www.experian.co.uk

There will be a nominal charge for your report, usually about £2, but you will be able to see immediately if your identity has been fraudulently used to set up any loans or credit accounts. When you receive your report, carefully review the contents and immediately close any unauthorised accounts. You will also be able to stop any pending applications, rectify your credit report and prevent fraudsters from continuing to use your identity. Depending on the nature of the entry to be rectified, this can be an arduous and time-consuming process but at least with your report as a starting point, you can contact the relevant companies to rectify your file. If you do need to make any changes, then make sure that you keep accurate and detailed records of all correspondence that is exchanged. This will help to resolve any issues that may occur at a later date.

In addition to supplying your credit file, these agencies also offer a range of subscription services that will monitor your report and contact you if there are any changes. Some services permit unlimited access to your report and will also send regular identity theft news together with advice and tips about how to protect yourself. For further information see:

MyCallcredit E-Alerts        www.mycallcredit.com
Equifax Credit Watch         www.equifax.co.uk
Experian CreditExpert        www.experian.co.uk

## TOP TEN TIPS TO IDENTIFY IF YOU ARE A VICTIM

✔ Invoices, receipts or statements are personally addressed to you for goods or services that you did not order or request.

✔ You receive letters from solicitors or debt recovery agencies for debts that are not yours.

✔ Confirmation letters are sent from companies referring to goods, services or accounts that you have not applied for.

✔ Review your credit report from one of the three credit reference agencies, Callcredit, Equifax or Experian, notify them of any new accounts or searches that you do not recognise and immediately close any compromised accounts.

✔ Carefully check your bank and card statements for any unusual or irregular transactions that you do not recognise and immediately report these to the respective company or organisation concerned.

✔ Important identity related post such as utility bills, bank statements, passports or driving licences have been lost or stolen.

✔ You are refused credit despite having a good credit rating or you apply for state benefits and are told that you are already claiming.

✔ Your post does not arrive. If this happens, contact Royal Mail to find out if a redirection notice has been issued against your address without your knowledge or permission.

✔ You suspect that your rubbish has been stolen or tampered with.

✔ Prepare an action plan of who to contact if your identity becomes compromised and keep this together with a list of emergency contact numbers.

## VICTIMS' STORIES

### CV identity fraud

When Joshua's car was broken into he noticed that besides his radio, CDs and an expensive coat, the thieves also took a copy of his CV. He reported the theft to the police but did not mention the CV because he thought it was just a piece of paper. Two months later, one of the referees from his CV received a letter from a large insurance company requesting a reference for Joshua. Fortunately, the referee knew that Joshua had not applied for a job at the company and declined the request.

The thief had used Joshua's CV to fraudulently apply for a job and if he had been successful then he could have used payslips to apply for credit or could have stolen customer account details. Joshua has since applied for a copy of his credit reference file and regularly checks this to see if any credit applications have been made in his name.

### Postal identity fraud

When Daniel and Laura moved to another part of the country they arranged to have their post redirected, notified the local authority that they would not be liable for council tax and had their names removed from the electoral roll. At first everything appeared to be fine but almost as soon as the redirection ended the frauds began. The first instance was when Laura received a telephone call from her previous neighbour who had accepted a mail order delivery in her name. Laura knew that she had not ordered the goods so she contacted the company and subsequently stopped a second order from being despatched. To prove she had moved, Laura had to send the company a copy of her birth certificate together with a letter from her solicitor.

Laura was advised to contact a credit reference agency, order a copy of her credit report and check for anything that she did not recognise. She noticed another mail order account with another company who regularly sent her brochures even though she had never ordered anything from them. The credit reference agency removed the fraudulent accounts and added a password-protected notice to her file. Now companies can only search Laura's file if she authorises them with her password. Laura has since registered with the mail preference service to stop any direct mail being delivered to her previous address in her name.

## (6)

# Reporting Identity Fraud

If you have, or suspect you may have, become a victim of identity fraud then it is important to act quickly to reduce the extent of the fraud. The first thing to remember is not to panic but to systematically contact each financial, utility and identity-related company that you deal with. This is why it is a good idea to keep a list of emergency contact numbers safely locked away for quick reference. The order in which you contact these companies will depend on the type of fraud that you have suffered. If you have Identity Fraud Insurance (see page 54, Identity Fraud Protection Services), then contact your insurance provider first. They will immediately assign an identity fraud expert who will help you to resolve the situation.

## CONTACTING THE POLICE

Following discussions between the financial industry and the Association of Chief Police Officers (ACPO), the Home Office has introduced a new reporting procedure for identity fraud involving online banking, cheques and credit or debit cards. With effect from 1 April 2007, it has been mutually agreed that in the first instance these types of frauds should be reported to the financial organisations involved and not directly to the police. The reason for this is to simplify the initial investigation and reporting process by reducing the level of bureaucracy involved in the recording of fraud. Under this new procedure, financial organisations are responsible for undertaking further investigation and, if necessary, reporting the fraud to the police on your behalf.

However, if your personal documents, credit cards or other identity-related items have been stolen, report the theft to the police and request a crime reference number. This number may be necessary to convince companies that your details have been fraudulently used to open accounts or apply for credit and other services in your name.

## CONTACTING OTHER ORGANISATIONS

Regardless of which identity-related fraud you have been a victim of, as a precautionary measure it is advisable to notify every company and organisation that you have an account with. These include:

- Driver and Vehicle Licensing Agency (DVLA)
- Identity and Passport Service (IPS)
- banks and building societies
- credit card companies
- utility providers (gas, electric, water, telephone)
- insurance companies
- Royal Mail.

Where possible you should cancel or freeze as many accounts as possible until the situation is fully resolved. If your credit or debit cards are protected (see page 35, Using Credit and Debit Cards Safely) then notify your insurance provider as soon as possible. They will arrange to cancel your cards and order replacements with new account numbers.

## KEEPING ACCURATE RECORDS

Reclaiming your identity and restoring your financial status can be a lengthy, time-consuming and emotionally draining experience. To help make this process a little less stressful it is important to keep detailed and accurate records. One of the best ways to do this is to create a comprehensive diary containing a full account of everything you did and everyone you wrote or spoke to. These records will be particularly useful to support your case if legal action is taken because you will be expected to prove that you are not responsible or liable for any accounts that have been fraudulently set up in your name. You will also need to prove what you have done to sort the problem out and how much time and money it has cost, because you may be able to recover these expenses.

When communicating with companies and organisations it is important to create a verifiable paper trail that can categorically prove what was said to whom and when. Emails are useful for this but they can be easily altered so they are not always relied upon in a court of law. Similarly, proving what was said in a telephone conversation can also be difficult. The most reliable way to exchange and confirm information is by letter, which should be sent by registered mail and copies should always be kept. In circumstances when an email or telephone call has been used to relay important information, ask the person concerned to confirm what they have said by letter. If this is not possible, then write to them and confirm your understanding of what was discussed and agreed.

## PROTECTIVE REGISTRATION FROM CIFAS

The Credit Industry Fraud Advisory Scheme (CIFAS) is a not-for-profit organisation who are dedicated to the prevention of financial crime. CIFAS do not provide a credit reference service but their information is used by fraud prevention agencies and credit reference agencies when fraudulent activity is suspected. They also exchange information about innocent fraud victims. So if your personal identification documents are stolen or if your identity has been fraudulently used then your personal details can be registered with the CIFAS Protective Registration service.

This service is provided by Equifax who will, for a nominal fee, assign a 'Category 0' against your name and address in their database which means that when CIFAS members conduct a credit search, they will see 'CIFAS – Do Not Reject – Refer For Validation' on your credit reference file. They will then need to contact Equifax to ascertain the reason for the entry and will request that further and more thorough identity checks are conducted before approval is granted.

Unless you write to Equifax to extend or cancel the service, Protective Registration will remain on your file for at least a year from the date of the most recent fraudulent activity. During this time you may find it takes longer for companies to process your credit applications but this is good because it proves that the service is working. This service can also be used by a relative or executor of a deceased person if there is reason to believe that their identity could by used by a criminal. When you apply to Equifax for the CIFAS Protective Registration service you will be asked to provide the following details:

- your full name
- your date of birth
- your full address and postcode
- the names and dates of birth of anyone else living at your address
- your home and work telephone numbers
- a crime reference number if applicable
- details about why you want a Protective Registration
- a copy of the death certificate if you are applying to protect the identity of a deceased person.

For further information, contact:

CIFAS Protective Registration Service
PO Box 1141, Bradford, BD1 5UR
Tel: 0870 010 2091
Email: protective.registrationuk@equifax.com

Equifax
Credit File Advice Centre, PO Box 1140, Bradford, BD1 5US
Tel: 0870 010 0583
www.equifax.co.uk

# Jargon Buster

**419 Scam** A type of advance fee fraud that originates from West Africa and is named after the section of the Nigerian legal code that relates to the crime.

**802.11** A standard for wireless networks that ensures compatibility between different manufacturers.

**Access point** A wireless hub that links together different 802.11 network cards to create an infrastructure wireless network.

**Ad-hoc network** A wireless network that connects computers on a peer-to-peer basis instead of routing traffic through a central access point.

**Advance fee fraud** Victims pay an upfront fee with the hope of receiving a large sum of money later.

**Adware** A type of spyware that causes unwanted adverts to be displayed on a computer.

**Anti-virus software** Software designed to detect and prevent known viruses.

**Attachments** Files, programs or documents that are attached to an email.

**Back door** A software loophole used by hackers to access a computer.

**Bin raiding** When criminals raid rubbish bins to gather personal information.

**Biometric verification** The use of fingerprints and irises as a means of identity authentication.

**BIOS and Boot Passwords** Passwords that prevent unauthorised users from starting a computer.

**Boot** The process of starting up or resetting a computer.

**Browser** A program used to access the internet.

**Card identity theft** When criminals use someone's identity to successfully apply for new credit cards or take over their existing accounts.

**Card-not-present (CNP) fraud** This occurs when a card is not required at the point of sale to complete a purchase such as through mail order, over the telephone or online.

**Card trapping devices** These thin devices are inserted into the card slot of cash machines to trap credit and debit cards.

**Chat rooms** Online discussion groups where users can chat in real time.

**Cookie** A small computer program used to record and relay information to the originating website about the user.

**Corporate identity crime** This describes the three main types of corporate identity related crimes which are corporate identity theft, creating a false corporate identity and committing corporate identity fraud.

**Corporate identity theft** When a genuine business is cloned and its name and credit accounts are used to fraudulently obtain goods, services and money which is known as corporate identity fraud.

**Counterfeit and cloned card fraud** This occurs when data from the magnetic strip of a genuine card is electronically copied (skimmed) onto a new fake blank card without the cardholder's knowledge.

**Cracker** A hacker who uses their skills for malicious purposes.

**Cracking** The act of uncovering passwords.

**Data Protection Act** This Act sets the legal framework for dealing with private information and data in the UK.

**Decryption** Converting encrypted data back into its original form.

**Desktop firewall** An individual firewall that works on a specific computer.

**Download** Transferring a file from one computer to another.

**Email attachment** See *Attachments.*

**Email filter** Software that scans and filters incoming emails.

**Encryption** Converting data into an unreadable form.

**False corporate identity** This is created when fictitious details are used to set up and register a business that does not exist.

**False identity theft** This is an identity that has never existed before, it can be created when a completely new identity is produced from counterfeit documents or when genuine documents are altered to create a fictitious identity.

**File sharing** Exchanging files over the internet with other users.

**Fingerprint recognition** See *biometric verification.*

**Firewall** This prevents unauthorised access to a computer or network.

**Freeloading** When unauthorised users use your wireless connection to access the internet.

**Hacker** Someone who uses their technical expertise to break into computer systems.

**Hardware firewall** Operates as a standalone device instead of using a software program on a computer.

**Identity crime** Describes the three main types of identity related crime that are committed against private individuals, identity theft, creating a false identity and committing identity fraud.

**Identity fraud** Describes crimes committed whereby a false or existing identity is used to fraudulently obtain goods or services.

**Identity theft** Occurs when criminals acquire enough of someone's personal details to either assume their entire identity or to create a new and fictitious identity based on their details.

**Javascript** A type of programming language used to make web pages more interactive.

**Key logger** A computer program or device used to record a user's keystrokes to capture their personal details.

**Lost or stolen card fraud** When a criminal poses as someone else to obtain goods and services with a lost or stolen card.

**MAC filtering** Uses the unique ID (MAC) address of a network card to permit access to a computer network.

**Macro** A small program that automates repetitive tasks.

**Macro virus** A virus that is released when a macro is enabled.

**MasterCard SecureCode** An online security system that enables an additional password to be assigned to a credit card, which will be required by participating websites when making a purchase.

**Network** A series of computers that are connected to one another.

**Padlock** A symbol in a web browser window to indicate that an encrypted connection is being used to communicate with a website and that the site has a valid security certificate.

**Patch** A software update to improve the performance of a program.

**Peer-to-peer (P2P)** A network to share and exchange files in which each computer can be both a server and a client.

**Pharming** When the DNS software of a website is altered so that users are redirected to a fake website even though they have entered the correct internet address in their browser.

**Phishing** Email recipients are encouraged to visit and enter usernames, passwords and other personal details at a fraudulent website.

**Pop-up** A small window that opens over a web page to display advertisements.

**Postal interception card fraud** Occurs when a new card is stolen in transit before the card company has been able to deliver it.

**Root kit** A set of tools and programs used by hackers to gain access to a computer and control it.

**Router** A device that controls the exchange of information within a network.

**Server** A computer that provides a service to other computers and programs over a network.

**Shoulder surfing** The use of observation techniques to see your PIN, password or other personal details.

**Skimming** Swiping the magnetic strip of a credit or debit card through a machine to capture the account information.

**Smurfing** Processing multiple financial transactions that are just below the threshold level to be reported to the authorities.

**Social engineering** A collection of techniques used by fraudsters to persuade people to divulge personal and confidential information.

**Software firewall** Runs on a computer as a program, as opposed to a hardware firewall that is a separate standalone device.

**Spam** Unsolicited junk emails.

**Spoof email** Fraudulent emails that appear to come from one user but have been sent by another.

**Spyware** Unwanted software programs that covertly monitor a user's activity, scan for personal information or enable outsiders to remotely control a computer.

**SSID** The Service Set Identifier is the name given to a wireless network that enables other users to find it.

**Strong passwords** These use the entire keyboard to create a random string of upper and lower case letters, numbers, keyboard symbols and punctuation marks.

**Trojan horse** A computer program that appears to perform one function but in reality performs another such as releasing a virus or installing a back door program for hackers.

**Verified by Visa** An online security system that enables an additional password to be assigned to a credit card, which will be required by participating websites when making a purchase.

**Virus** Malicious programs that are designed to replicate themselves and spread from computer to computer by infecting other files, see *Trojan horse* and *Spyware*.

**Virus signature** A fingerprint that is used by anti-virus software to identify and detect an infection.

**WEP** Wired Equivalent Privacy is a type of wireless encryption that is usually found on older network cards. WEP is generally considered the weakest type of security because it uses numerical passwords which are relatively easy to crack.

# Useful Addresses

## Banking advice

APACS (The UK Payments Association), Mercury House, Triton Court, 14 Finsbury Square, London, EC2A 1LQ. Tel: 020 7711. 6200. Fax: 020 7256 5527. Email: corpcomms@apas.org.uk www.apacs.org.uk

Bank Safe Online, c/o APACS, Mercury House, Triton Court, 14 Finsbury Square, London, EC2A 1LQ. www.banksafeonline.org.uk

British Bankers' Association (BBA), Pinners Hall, 105–108 Old Broad Street, London, EC2N 1EX. Email: info@bba.org.uk www.bba.org.uk

Financial Services Authority (FSA), 25 The North Colonnade, Canary Wharf, London, E14 5HS. www.fsa.gov.uk

## Credit reports and reference agencies

Callcredit Limited, One Park Lane, Leeds, LS3 1EP. Automated Helpline: 0870 060 1414. Tel: 0113 244 1555. Fax: 0113 234 0050. www.callcredit.co.uk www.mycallcredit.com

Check My File, Credit Reporting Agency Limited, 13 High Cross, Truro, TR1 2AJ. Tel: 0800 612 0421. Fax: 0870 094 0069. www.checkmyfile.com

Equifax, Credit File Advice Centre, PO Box 1140, Bradford, BD1 5US. Tel: 0870 010 0583. www.equifax.co.uk

Experian, Consumer Help Service, PO Box 9000, Nottingham, NG80 7WP. Tel: 0870 241 6212. www.experian.co.uk

## Card protection services

Card Protection Plan (CPP), Holgate Park, York, YO26 4GA. Tel: 0870 600 3022 (Card Protection). Tel: 0870 121 9187 (Identity Protection). www.cpp.co.uk

Sentinel Card Protection, FREEPOST PT391, Portsmouth, PO3 5BR. Tel: 0800 414 717. www.sentinelcardprotection.com

## Identity fraud protection advice

CardWatch, c/o APACS, Mercury House, Triton Court, 14 Finsbury Square, London, EC2A 1LQ. www.cardwatch.org.uk

CIFAS (Credit Industry Fraud Advisory Scheme), 4th Floor, Central House, 14 Upper Woburn Place, London, WC1H 0NN. www.cifas.org.uk

CIFAS Protective Registration Service (provided by Equifax). Tel: 0870 010 2091. Email: protective.registrationuk@equifax.com

## Reporting identity fraud

City of London Police Fraud Desk. Tel: 020 7601 6999. Email: frauddesk@cityoflondon.pnn.police.uk

Crimestoppers, Apollo House, 66A London Road, Morden, Surrey, SM4 5BE. Tel: 0800 555 111. www.crimestoppers-uk.org

## Government agencies and departments

Driver and Vehicle Licensing Agency, DVLA, Swansea, SA6 7JL. Tel: 0870 240 0009. www.dvla.gov.uk

Identity and Passport Service (IPS). Tel: 0870 521 0410. www.passport.gov.uk

The Information Commissioner's Office (ICO), Wycliffe House, Water Lane, Wilmslow, Cheshire, SK9 5AF. Tel: 0845 630 6060 or 01625 545745. Fax: 01625 524510. Email: mail@ico.gsi.gove.uk www.ico.gov.uk

## Reducing sales and marketing information

The Bereavement Register, Freepost, SEA8240, Sevenoaks, TN13 1YR. Tel: 0870 600 7222. Fax: 0870 400 5644. Email: help@the-bereavement-register.com www.the-bereavement-register.org.uk

Deceased Preference Service (DPS), Windhill Manor, Leeds Road, Shipley, BD18 1BP. Tel: 0800 068 4433. www.deceasedpreferenceservice.co.uk

Email Preference Service (eMPS) www.dmachoice.org/EMPS/

Fax Preference Service (FPS), 3rd Floor, DMA House, 70 Margaret Street, London, W1W 8SS. FPS Registration Line: 0845 070 0702. Tel: 0845 703 4599. Fax: 020 7323 4226. Email: fps@dma.org.uk www.fpsonline.org.uk

Mail Preference Service (MPS), FREEPOST 29 LON20771, London, W1E 0ZT. MPS Registration Line: 0845 703 4599. Tel: 0845 703 4599. Fax: 020 7323 4226. Email: mps@dma.org.uk www.mpsonline.org.uk

Telephone Preference Service (TPS), 3rd Floor, DMA House, 70 Margaret Street, London, W1W 8SS. TPS Registration Line: 0845 070 0707. Tel: 0845 703 4599. Fax: 020 7323 4226. Email: tps@dma.org.uk www.tpsonline.org.uk

## Identity fraud protection services

Formations House, 29 Harley Street, London, W1G 9QR.
Tel: 0207 016 2727. Fax: 020 7637 0419.
Email: info@formationshouse.com
www.formationshouse.com

Identitycare. Tel: 0870 606 4050 www.identitycare.co.uk

ID Theft Protect, PO Box 879, Peterborough, PE1 9BU.
Tel: 0870 766 9234. www.id-protect.co.uk

Protect My Company, Matthew House, Matthew Street,
Dunstable, LU6 1SD. Tel: 0845 400 0777.
Email: Admin@ProtectMyCompany.co.uk
www.protectmycompany.co.uk

Royal Mail Customer Enquiry, Customer Services, Freepost, RM1 1AA. Tel: 0845 774 0740.
www.royalmail.com

## Online shopping

Shopsafe, c/o Edward Robertson, 1 Bongate, Darlington,
DL3 7JA. Tel: 01325 489 3000.
Email: info@shopsafe.co.uk www.shopsafe.co.uk

# Useful Identify Fraud Protection Websites

**Advice UK** – www.adviceuk.org.uk

A network of advice providing organisations.

**Advicenow** – www.advicenow.org.uk

Advicenow is an independent, not-for-profit website providing accurate, up-to-date information on rights and legal issues.

**Anti-Phishing Working Group** – www.antiphishing.org

Cross-industry global group supporting those tackling phishing and pharming by providing advice on anti-phishing controls and information on current trends.

**APACS** – www.apacs.org.uk

Association for Payment Clearing Services (APACS), is the UK trade association for the banking industry that provides a forum for its members to come together on non-competitive issues relating to the payments industry. They also work with police, retailers, cardholders and organisations to fight payment card fraud.

**Association of Chief Police Officers (ACPO)** –

www.acpo.police.uk

ACPO works in equal and active partnership with Government and the Association of Police Authorities to lead and coordinate the direction and development of the police service in England, Wales and Northern Ireland.

**Bank Safe Online** – www.banksafeonline.org.uk

Bank Safe Online is run by APACS on behalf of its member banks to help online banking customers stay safe online.

**British Bankers' Association** – www.bba.org.uk

The British Bankers' Association is the leading trade association in the UK financial services industry. Its 220 members, banks and other financial services firms, fund its not-for-profit activities.

**Card Watch** – www.cardwatch.org.uk

Card Watch raises awareness about all types of plastic card fraud in the UK and provides information to prevent fraudulent use of credit cards, debit cards, cheque guarantee cards and charge cards.

**Check My File** – www.checkmyfile.com

Check My File can provide your credit score, credit rating and neighbourhood data for free, plus online credit reports, expert credit file analysis and monitoring, vehicle checks and pension checks.

**Citizens Advice** – www.adviceguide.org.uk

An online version of the Citizens Advice Bureau providing independent advice on your rights.

**Consumer Direct** – www.consumerdirect.gov.uk

A government funded telephone and online advice service operated by the Office of Fair Trading (OFT) providing clear, practical advice on a wide range of consumer issues. The advice is free and you can call 0845 404 0506 as many times as you need to.

**Dedicated Cheque and Plastic Crime Unit (DCPCU)** –
www.dcpcu.org.uk
The DCPCU is sponsored by APACS on behalf of the
banking industry. It comprises a group of specialist
police officers and civilian staff to tackle the organised
gangs responsible for much of the UK's card and
cheque fraud.

**Get Safe Online** – www.getsafeonline.org.uk
Protect yourself from identity thieves, viruses, phishing and other internet threats with expert advice from
the British Government, the Serious and Organised
Crime Agency and industry specialists will help you
guard against online dangers.

**HM Revenue & Customs** – www.hmrc.gov.uk
HMRC is responsible for collecting the bulk of tax
revenue, as well as paying Tax Credits and Child
Benefits, and strengthening the UK's frontiers.

**Home Office** – www.homeoffice.gov.uk
Provides advice and information about the work of
the Home Office and also provides links to other
government departments.

**Home Office Identity Fraud Steering Committee** –
www.identitytheft.org.uk
A collaboration between UK financial bodies, government and the police to combat the threat of identity
theft.

**How To Wipe Your Hard Drive** –
www.howtowipeyourdrive.com
Useful advice about safely removing data from your
Windows, Macintosh or Unix hard drive.

**Identity and Passport Service** – www.ips.gov.uk
The official website for the Home Office department

responsible for issuing UK passports and ID cards.

**Foreign and Commonwealth Office** – www.fco.gov.uk
British government department responsible for overseas relations and foreign affairs through its headquarters in London and its Embassies, High Commissions and Consulates throughout the world.

**Financial Service Authority (FSA)** – www.fsa.gov.uk
Regulator of all providers of financial services in the UK, the Bank of England retains responsibility for systemic risk.

**Fraud Watch International** –
www.fraudwatchinternational.com
Combines anti-phishing education, monitoring and detection services and preventative software solutions to consumers and corporate clients.

**Microsoft Security At Home** –
www.microsoft.com/security/protect
Useful help and advice to protect your computer, yourself and your family from online threats and inappropriate content and contact.

**Miller Smiles** – www.millersmiles.co.uk
A large archive of spoof email and phishing scams.

**Office of Fair Trading (OFT)** – www.oft.gov.uk
The OFT enforces UK consumer protection law and competition law, reviews proposed mergers and conducts market studies.

**Serious Organised Crime Agency (SOCA)** –
www.soca.gov.uk
Non-geographic police unit responsible for undertaking pro-active operations against serious and organised crime.

**Spamfo** – www.spamfo.co.uk

Organised collection of news, reviews and links about unsolicited bulk email (spam).

**Shop Safe Online** – www.shopsafeonline.org.uk

Provides information about registering and using MasterCard SecureCode and Verified by Visa.

**Shopsafe UK** – www.shopsafe.co.uk

A UK online shopping directory listing secure UK online shops so you can shop on the internet with confidence. The site also includes special offers, gift ideas and safe shopping advice.

**Stay Safe Online** – www.staysafeonline.info

Provides free and non-technical cyber security and safety resources to the public, so consumers, small businesses and educators have the know-how to avoid cyber crime.

**Trading Standards Central** –

www.tradingstandards.gov.uk

A one-stop shop for consumer protection information in the UK. The site is supported and maintained by the Trading Standards Institute (TSI).

# Index

## 7 Ways for Anyone to Boost their Income
*How making a few simple changes can significantly reduce your outgoings and gain extra income*
**Anthony Vice**

The chances are that you are paying too much interest on your mortgage, or paying the wrong amount of tax, or too much insurance – if so, you need this book. In it, Anthony Vice outlines simple but effective ways to make you better off. They don't involve any drastic changes to your lifestyle – just some painless alterations in procedure that will significantly reduce your outgoings – so that you keep more of your income to save or spend on the things you really want. Anthony's advice is for all age groups – and the sooner you start, the more you'll save.

ISBN 978-1-84528-239-4

## How To Save Inheritance Tax
*Understand how inheritance tax works – and pass on more of your hard-earned wealth to those you love*
Gordon Bowley LLB

Although inheritance tax is a technical and increasingly complex subject, this book is intended to give the non-lawyer a thorough, working understanding of the tax. It points out steps that can be taken to ensure that hard-earned wealth can be passed to those they care for, rather than leaving it for the state to dissipate. This book will enable readers to assess their particular situation and discover where it might be considerably improved and talk with advisers intelligently; judge their worth; and evaluate their advice.

ISBN 978-1-84528-260-8

# How To Pay Less for More

*The Consumer's Guide to Negotiating the Best Deals – Whatever You're Buying*

'This book could save you thousands!'

Marc Lockley

This book will give you the skills to negotiate better deals in every area of your life. Marc Lockley, Negotiation Coach, teaches the basic negotiation skills and applies them to common situations that we all experience, either at home or in the workplace: buying a car, buying or selling a house, booking a holiday, planning a wedding or party, buying electrical goods, buying and fitting kitchens and bathrooms, complaining effectively and negotiating a pay rise or flexible hours. Marc estimates that by using the skills he teaches he saves himself thousands of pounds each year and has a higher standard of living than he might otherwise expect.

ISBN 978-1-84528-237-0

# How To Get Good Care Services

*for yourself or your relatives*
Clare Kirkman

Care services are expanding and more organisations are opening, providing a better range of choice. Greater competition is pushing up standards of service and bringing better value for money. The tighter regulation of care services and improved quality control methods are increasing the power of consumers. As a modern consumer of care services you must take control of the process, whether the care is for you or for a loved one. This book explains where you can find care services and how to recognise quality care when you find it. It explains what you can expect in terms of the standard of care and service; and what you can do if you don't get it.

ISBN 978-1-84528-243-1

**How to feed your whole family a healthy, balanced diet, with very little money and hardly any time, even if you have a tiny kitchen, only three saucepans (one with an ill-fitting lid) and no fancy gadgets – unless you count the garlic crusher ...**
*Simple, wholesome and nutritious recipes for family meals*
Gill Holcombe

This book provides simple, wholesome and nutritious recipes for family meals; quick lunches, tasty puddings and cakes – and you don't have to spend hours slaving over a hot stove, or spend a fortune at the supermarket. There are menu plans, recipes, shortcuts and dozens of ideas for every meal, together with tried and tested tips to help you save your valuable time and money. Gill Holcombe is passionate about feeding her kids good food. She grew up before the culture of convenience food took hold – and knows how to cook. Having brought up three children on her own for over ten years, she says the proof of the pudding is in the eating, and has three fit, healthy teenagers with loads of energy – and no fillings in their teeth.

ISBN 978-1-905862-15-3

## The Parent's Guide to Childcare
*How to choose the right childcare for you and your child*
Allison Lee

This book looks at the most popular types of childcare available and weighs up the advantages and disadvantages of each to help you to decide which service suits you best. It will help you to decide what kind of childcare you require; ensure that the relationship between the child and the carer and you and the carer work well; know what to expect from your childminder in terms of play and educational activities; know what to do when either your child or the carer is ill; understand the childcare contract and know what to do when things go wrong.

ISBN 978-1-84528-220-2

How To Books are available through all good bookshops, or you can order direct from us through Grantham Book Services.

Tel: +44 (0)1476 541080
Fax: +44 (0)1476 541061
Email: *orders@gbs.tbs-ltd.co.uk*

Or via our website

*www.howtobooks.co.uk*

To order via any of these methods please quote the title(s) of the book(s) and your credit card number together with its expiry date.

For further information about our books and catalogue, please contact:

How To Books
Spring Hill House
Spring Hill Road
Begbroke
Oxford
OX5 1RX

Visit our web site at

*www.howtobooks.co.uk*

Or you can contact us by email at info@howtobooks.co.uk